# Let's Talk About God

## Devotions for families with young children

## Margaret J. Anderson

**BETHANY FELLOWSHIP, INC.**
Minneapolis, Minnesota

*Let's Talk About God*
by Margaret J. Anderson

Library of Congress Catalog Card Number 75-6055

ISBN 0-87123-340-1

Published by Bethany Fellowship, Inc.
6820 Auto Club Road, Minneapolis, Minnesota 55438

Printed in the United States of America

*Dedicated
to Robin, Paul and Hope*

The pictures appearing on pages 71, 105 and 133 are used through the courtesy of John Thornberg. All other pictures are used through the courtesy of Bonnie E. Sampson.

# Preface

When children gathered around Jesus He took them into His arms and blessed them. When His disciples objected because they felt He was being imposed upon, He said, "Let the children come to me. . . ."

To you, *parent, teacher, pastor, missionary,* Jesus reiterates this admonition: *let the children come to me.* To facilitate this coming you will spend time with children. You will listen to them. You will guide and teach them.

According to God's Word,* they will never be more receptive to Bible truths than they are now. Be assured, too, that faith established in childhood will not, in the final analysis, be discarded at an older age.

This book is written prayerfully (and with gratefulness to friends who shared anecdotes involving children) as a sequel to *Happy Moments with God,** another book of devotionals written for families with young children and for individuals who work with youth.

Margaret J. Anderson

---

* The Scripture passages are paraphrases from several translations.
** Also a Bethany Fellowship, Inc., publication.

# Table of Contents

# A New Song

Steve could hardly wait for his cousin Paul to arrive for a visit. *I wonder what he'll think of Blaze now?* Steve thought. Blaze was Steve's canary. He had bought him for twenty-five cents at an auction after old Mr. MacDougal, the hermit, died.

At that time Blaze was the scruffiest, saddest canary in the whole world. When he sang, he made strange, squawking noises. Paul, who had been visiting him then, laughed at him for paying a quarter for such a sad bird. Well, he'd show him.

When Paul arrived and saw Blaze, he let out a long, low whistle.

"Wow! Is that the same bird?"

"Yup," Steve answered. Then he told his cousin how he had scrubbed the cage, how he had fed and groomed the bird.

"Well, I never . . . " Paul began.

At that very moment Blaze burst into song. "How did he learn to sing like that?" Paul asked, surprise in his voice.

Steve didn't answer. Instead, he walked over to the stereo and put on a record played by the London Symphony Orchestra. Blaze cocked his head—listening. Then he threw back his head, fluffed his feathers, opened his mouth, and began to sing, matching every pause and every high note of the orchestra.

"I can't believe it," Paul said. "Want to sell him?"

"My twenty-five-cent canary?" Steve teased. "You want *him*?" He pretended he was thinking about it. Then

11

he shook his head. "Not on your life. Not now."

*Something to Think About:* What made the canary change?

Did you know that people, too, can change like that?

When a person realizes that Jesus loves him he changes. He understands he is important to Jesus. He cleans up his life. He takes a new interest in people. He looks different. He smiles. Yes, he even sings a new song.

*Bible Verse:* "Therefore if any man be in Christ, he is a new creature: old things are passed away; behold, all things are become new" (2 Cor. 5:17).

*Prayer:* We praise and thank you, Lord, for being the kind of Savior you are. Thank you for changing people. Thank you for making them new. Thank you for putting a new song in their hearts. Help us to show that we belong to you because we have changed. Amen.

## No One Like You

Blenda enjoyed looking at the baby book in which her mother had kept a record of her life from the time she was born. In it Mother had pasted pictures of Blenda at different ages. The first one was taken in the hospital. Blenda found it hard to believe she had ever been that small.

Next was a picture of Mother and Father leaving the hospital with their baby. Later there were pictures of Blenda taking her first steps; eating with a spoon for the first time; visiting Grandma and Grandpa. Blenda liked the pictures taken at Christmas time best of all.

One day when Blenda was examining the baby book, her mother showed her the birth certificate the doctor filled out when she was born. On it were two small footprints.

"Do all birth certificates have footprints on them?" Blenda asked.

"Now all of them do."

"Why?"

"When you were born the nurse put a name tag on your wrist so you wouldn't be mistaken for anyone else's baby. To be doubly sure, your little feet were placed on an ink pad, then on the birth certificate to prove you are you."

"They're so tiny."

"They surely are. But what is more important is that they are different from anyone else's. And just as footprints differ, fingerprints differ too. No two are ever exactly alike. Even voice patterns vary. If our voice patterns were recorded by a machine made for that purpose, we would

13

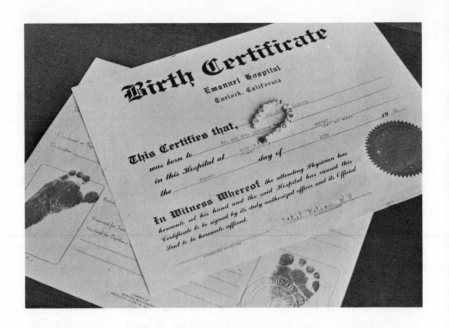

find that mine is different from yours."

Blenda thought for a while. Then she exclaimed, "Wow! Isn't God wonderful?"

*Something to Think About:* If there are several children in your family, check footprint differences on your birth certificates.

Now talk about God as the great creator. Name some of the different kinds of flowers He has made. Name as many different kinds of animals and birds as you can. Talk about the stars, the sun, and the moon. Check an encyclopedia to see how far they are from the earth. Think about the fact that they hang in space with nothing to support them.

*Bible Verse:* "God made and fashioned me. . ." (Ps. 119:73).

"You, even you, are Lord alone. You made the heaven with all its stars and planets. You made the earth and everything on it; the seas and all that live in them. You keep everything in control" (Neh. 9:6).

"God hangs the earth on nothing" (Job 26:7).

"Every day will I bless your name; I will praise you forever and ever" (Ps. 145:2).

"I will bless the Lord at all times; his praise shall be on my lips at all times" (Ps. 34:1).

*Prayer:* Dear God, we feel like Blenda did. We say, "Wow! Isn't God wonderful?" We thank you and praise you for making such a marvelous world. Thank you for making each one of us different. Thank you for giving us minds to learn about you and your world. Thank you for giving us tongues so we *can* thank and praise you for what you have done. Amen.

## He Knows Your Name

"I don't like our new teacher," Sara told her mother shortly after school had begun one fall.

"Careful, dear," Mother answered. "You haven't known her very long."

"It's been over a week, and she still doesn't know who we are. She always says, 'You, in the yellow dress. . . .' Or 'You in the red sweater over there. . . .'"

*Something to Think About:* Like Sara we like to have people remember our names. We feel they care for and love us if they do.

Well, one thing we can depend on is that God knows our name. He knows the number of stars and He knows all of their names. He knows when the tiniest sparrow falls to the ground.

Jesus said, "I am the good shepherd. I know my sheep."

When we think of ourselves as Jesus' sheep, we should

15

remember that He knows the names of each of us. We can be sure He will never forget them because He has a record of them in heaven.

*Bible Verse:* "And the sheep hear his voice and he calls his own sheep by name" (John 10:3).

"Rejoice because your names are written in heaven" (Luke 10:20).

*Prayer:* Dear Lord, thank you for caring for each one of us. You know what we think. You know the mistakes we make. You know when we get discouraged. Yet you always love us. Help us to love each other the way you do. Amen.

# Three Persons in One

"God is triune. He is three persons in one. He is God the Father, Jesus the Son, and He is the Holy Spirit."

David had heard his pastor say this many times. *"Trinity . . . triune God . . . three in one."* He just didn't understand it at all—until one day when his missionary uncle, a doctor in Zaire, Africa, visited his home.

"How can this be?" he asked his uncle.

"I don't think anyone really understands exactly what the word *trinity* means," his uncle told him. "That's because we too often think of God as having a body like ours. The Bible says, 'God is a spirit: and they that worship him must worship him in spirit and in truth.' When God made us in His own image He gave us a spirit like His.

"Now," he continued, "tell me what I do in Africa."

"You work in a hospital. You make people well."

"That's right. At the hospital I am a doctor. What else do I do?"

"You preach to the Africans on Sundays."

"Okay, I'm a doctor and I'm a preacher. But I am also a father. When I come home after a busy day, I read to my children. I play games with them. I help them with their homework. So you see, in a way, I am three persons in one, too."

David nodded. *Father, doctor, preacher,* he thought; *three persons in one.*

*Something to Think About:* What three persons is God?

God the Father is the creator and ruler of the world.

God the Son is the Savior of the world.

God the Holy Spirit is the Spirit of God who lives in all people who ask Him to come into their lives.

*Bible Verse:* "But the Comforter [the Holy Spirit], whom the Father [God] will send in my [Jesus'] name, he shall teach you all things" (John 14:26).

"The grace [the blessing] of the Lord Jesus Christ, and the love of God, and the communion [fellowship] of the Holy Spirit, be with you all. Amen" (2 Cor. 13:14).

*Prayer:* Thank you for this story, Lord. Thank you for being Father, Son, and Holy Spirit. Now we understand a little better what trinity means.

Fill our lives with your Spirit. We need His help in understanding all that the Bible tells us. Amen.

## Life Is Like a Jigsaw Puzzle

Little Sue asked her sister, Jodi, and her brother, Paul, to help her put her new jigsaw puzzle together. Jodi and Paul were delighted. Jigsaw puzzles were fun!

Jodi dumped the puzzle pieces on the table and spread them face down so the picture pattern was hidden. Then she and Paul went right to work. Sue helped for a time, but she soon grew tired of the puzzle. *I'll get my doll,* she thought. *But first,* she giggled, *I'll play a trick on Jodi and Paul.*

When they weren't looking she slipped four of the puzzle pieces into her dress pocket. Then she went to get her doll. She pulled up a rocker and began to rock the doll. In a very short time she forgot all about the puzzle. Until . . .

"Susan Anne!" Paul said crossly. "Four puzzle pieces are missing. Have you been up to one of your tricks?"

Sue closed her eyes and kept on rocking her doll.

"Susan, how do you expect us to finish the puzzle if we don't have all the pieces?" Jodi asked. "Give them to me."

Slowly Sue's hand moved toward her dress pocket. She reached in, found the puzzle parts and handed them to Jodi. She threw back her head and laughed and laughed.

Jodi and Paul didn't think she was funny.

"Dumb kid!" Paul said as he shook his finger in her face. Then in a more playful voice, he added, "Stupid, silly little sister! She doesn't know it takes all the pieces to make a puzzle picture."

*Something to Think About:* You already know that God has a plan for your life. Right now that plan might seem like a puzzle to you. But, God knows where every piece belongs. He can put them all together if . . . If what?

Jesus said, "Give me your heart." How much of it does He want?

*Bible Verse:* "Thou shalt love the Lord thy God with *all* thy heart, and with *all* thy soul, and with *all* thy mind" (Matt. 22:37).

*Prayer* (to be prayed in unison): Dear Jesus, not just a part, but all of my heart—I want to give all to you. Amen.

## Hide God's Word in Your Heart

In several instances when our soldiers were captured by the Communists, all their personal belongings were taken away from them—even their Bibles. Not to have a Bible was hard on the soldiers who loved God's holy book.

But these were clever men. They have told us how they managed to get a Bible. In secret, on scraps of paper (often toilet paper), each man wrote down the Bible verses he had memorized when he was young (the Ten Commandments, the Twenty-third Psalm, 1 Corinthians 13, the First Psalm, favorite verses of all kinds).

When all of these verses were put together, the prisoners had their own little Bible which they passed around, always guarding it carefully. They knew the guards would take it away from them if it was found.

When released many of these soldiers said their secret Bible was the thing that gave them the hope and comfort they so badly needed while in prison.

*Something to Think About:* In many countries today people are treated like the prisoners were. They aren't allowed to have Bibles, either. If Bibles are found, their owners are often arrested and punished.

How much do you love your Bible?

How big a Bible would your family have if all that was in it were the Bible verses you had memorized?

Try to memorize a few verses every week. Then if your Bible is taken away from you, you will have one of your own, stored in your mind.

*Bible Verse:* "My son, if you will take my words, and hide them [memorize them] . . . you will learn to know about God's wisdom" (Prov. 2:1-5).

"Your [God's] word have I hid in my heart so I won't sin against you" (Ps. 119:11).

"Therefore you should put these words in your heart [memorize them]" (Deut. 11:18).

"Your word is pure, that's why I love it" (Ps. 119:140).

*Prayer:* Dear Lord God, thank you for giving us the Bible which tells us about you and your plan to send Jesus into the world so we could learn about you. Forgive us for not memorizing it as we should. Help us to want to hide it in our hearts. Amen.

## God Is Everywhere

Boyd watched his family's furniture being loaded into the truck. His father was going to drive it when they left for California later that day, and his mother would drive the family car. Boyd was excited because his parents had promised him that he could ride in the truck part of the time.

The packers wrapped each piece of furniture in a thick blanket to keep it from being scratched along the way. They knew just where to put each one in the truck.

Finally everything was ready. The suitcases with the clothes the family would need on the trip were put in the trunk of the car. Boyd and his parents said good-bye to relatives and friends who had come to see them off. Then his father climbed into the truck; Boyd and his mother, into the car.

When they drove away Boyd knelt on the back seat of the car and waved to the people who stood watching them. "Good-bye, Gram. Good-bye, Gramps. Good-bye, Uncle Phil," he called even though he knew they could no longer hear him. Then just as the car turned the corner he added, "Good-bye, God, we're moving to California now."

*Something to Think About*: What's wrong with this story?

Does God live in only one city or town?

It seems Boyd didn't understand this, nor did he understand that he and his parents would need God's care and help on the trip and in their new home. One family who travels a great deal never starts their car each morning without first bowing their heads and asking God to protect them during that day.

*Bible Verse:* "The eyes of the Lord are in every place" (Prov. 15:3).

"If we seek God we can find him, for he is never far from any one of us" (Acts 17:27).

*Prayer:* Dear Lord, we are so glad that you are everywhere and that we don't need to hunt for you. We can talk to you any time and know that you can hear. Thank you for being everywhere. Amen.

## "I Won't Do It!"

Jimmy's Sunday school teacher gave him a recitation to learn for the church Christmas program.

"I won't say it," he told his parents. "I won't get up in front of the whole church and say what she wants me to say."

"Don't you think you can learn the recitation?" his father asked. Jimmy frowned. He already knew every word he was supposed to say. Did his father think he was stupid or something? He'd show him. In a loud, clear voice he said, "I'm just a little boy, but I know that Jesus was born on Christmas Day."

"Why, that's wonderful," Mother told him. "Then there's no reason why you shouldn't say it in church!"

Jimmy shook his head. "I won't do it." No amount of coaxing could get him to change his mind.

But the night of the program when his name was called, Jimmy marched to the platform. Mother and Dad couldn't believe their eyes.

Loud and clear Jimmy said, "I am a big boy, and I know that Jesus was born on Christmas Day."

*Something to Think About:* Did you notice how Jimmy changed his recitation?

Why do you think he didn't want to say he was a little boy?

It really doesn't matter whether he was big or little; the thing that matters is what he said he believed about Jesus.

When Jesus lived on earth He loved little children because their faith in Him was often greater than that of grownups. When He talked about faith He said everyone who comes to Him must have the same kind of faith as children have.

*Bible Verse:* "Except you have the faith a small child has, you will never enter the kingdom of God" (Matt. 18:3).

*Prayer:* Dear Jesus, we love you. We believe you were born in Bethlehem on a day we celebrate as Christmas Day. Help us not to be afraid to tell people we believe you are the Son of God who came to earth to tell us how we could become members of your kingdom. Amen.

# Camouflage

One of the most interesting things about God's world is the way some creatures can change their colors to blend with their surroundings. This blending is called *camouflage*. Camouflage makes an animal hard to see.

Many animals of the north turn white in winter. It is hard to see them because they look so much like the snow. The spotted fawn (young deer) of the white-tale deer family is so much like the woods it lives in that it is hard to see.

The chameleon is a kind of lizard. It changes its color to match its surroundings, too. Some chameleons change color in a few seconds. Shrimp can take on the color of the seaweeds in which they live.

*Something to Think About:* Some people are like these creatures. They take on the qualities of people they are with. Such a person may blend into certain surroundings so you really don't know what kind of person he is. When he is with one group of people, he is like them. When he is with others, he becomes like them. A boy may come to church and act like a Christian. Then he may go out with a gang of boys who are bad and do what they do.

Does God want us to camouflage our lives, to change our "color" and be different each time we are with different people? Or does He expect us to be the same all the time? Give the reason for your answer.

*Bible Verse:* "Therefore, you should be steadfast [not changing], unmovable [courageous, standing firm], always doing the work of the Lord, for you know that you will be rewarded by God" (1 Cor. 15:58).

"Stand fast in Christ, don't get tangled with the enemies of God" (Gal. 5:1).

"Because you know these things, be careful so you aren't coaxed away by wicked people" (2 Pet. 3:17).

"As my father [God] has loved me [Jesus], so have I loved you. Continue [stay], in my love" (John 15:9).

*Prayer:* Dear Lord God, thank you for staying true to us. Thank you for never changing your "color." Help us not to be chameleon Christians who are one thing one day and another the next. Keep us close to you at all times. Amen.

# Come in, Jesus

A picture painted by a famous artist shows Jesus as He stands knocking outside a closed door. There is no door-knob or latch on the outside of the door.

When Andre Vierra saw the picture for the first time, he stood and looked at it for several minutes. "Whose house is it?" he asked his mother.

Mrs. Vierra told her son that the artist painted the picture to show that "a person's heart—his life—is like the door. The latch is on the inside. Only he (or she) can open the door and invite Jesus to come in."

"Do people shut the door after Jesus comes in?" Andre wanted to know.

"I think that would be a good idea," Mrs. Vierra answered. "That would show they wanted Jesus to stay."

*Something to Think About:* When you invite Jesus into your heart, you will want to close the door, too. Because, as Mrs. Vierra said, you will want Him to live with you always. You will close the door, also, because you want to shut sin out.

If you have never done this, you can do it right now.

*Bible Verse:* "Whoever will call upon the Lord [invite him into their hearts] shall be saved" (Rom. 10:13).

"If you confess [tell others] you love Jesus and believe in your heart that God raised him from the dead, you will be saved" (Rom. 10:9).

*Prayer:*

Come into our hearts, Lord Jesus.
Come in today,
Come in to stay,

Come into our hearts, Lord Jesus.
Forgive our sins and help us to live for you
   always.
Amen.

## Show and Tell

Sally couldn't go to sleep. Tomorrow was her turn to "show and tell," and she didn't know what to show and tell. *Maybe Jesus can help me*, she thought. She began to pray, "Dear Jesus, help me think of something I can show and tell tomorrow. Amen."

She went to sleep. As soon as she awakened the next morning she thought of something she had forgotten all about. "I'll take it to school," she told herself. And that's what she did.

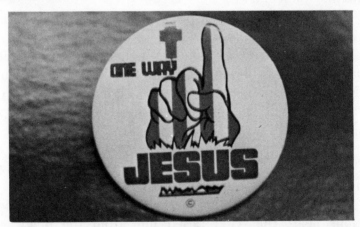

When the teacher called her name, Sally walked to the front of the room. She took a big round button pin out of her pocket. On it was a picture of a hand with one finger pointing straight up. Below the hand were the words: ONE WAY.

Sally showed the button to her classmates. Then she

said, "My brother got this button at a young people's meeting at church. He said I could have it. See the hand with one finger pointing up? That means there is only one way to heaven."

"How do you know?" one of the boys asked.

"Because Jesus said so, in the Bible." Sally answered.

"Thank you, Sally; now you may return to your seat," the teacher told her.

Later when school was dismissed, the teacher asked Sally not to leave right away. When they were alone, the teacher said, "Where do you go to church, Sally?"

Sally told her.

Then the teacher said, "I am new in town. I've been wondering where I should go to church. Now I know."

"Where?" Sally asked.

"I think I'd like to attend your church," the teacher answered.

*Something to Think About:* What do you think about Sally's show and tell?

Have you ever seen a ONE-WAY button?

Why do you think the teacher said she'd like to go to Sally's church?

Have you ever told anyone there is only one way to heaven? Should you?

*Bible Verse:* "I am the door; by me [Jesus] if any man enter in he will be saved" (John 10:9).

"I am the way, the truth, and the life; no man cometh to the father, but by me" (John 14:6).

*Prayer:* Dear God in heaven, thank you for sending your son to teach us that the right way to heaven is believing in Him. Thank you for mothers and fathers who teach us to love you. Thank you for our Sunday school teachers and our minister who help us learn about you too. Amen.

## She Already Knowed

At Bible school Trent learned that God is love. He learned that God loves us so much He sent His son to earth so we could learn to love and serve Him. He learned that because Jesus died on the cross, we have a right to ask Him to forgive our sins.

On the third day Trent's teacher had her children learn John 3:16, the verse that tells how much God loves us. When school was over, the teacher said, "I want you to go home and tell your parents that God loves them."

The next day she asked the children what their parents had said when they told them God loved them. "Trent, will you tell us what your mother said?"

Trent smiled happily. "She already knowed," he told the teacher.

*Something to Think About:* Do all people know God loves them?

What are some of the ways people can learn about God's love?

Do you know people who don't know God loves them?

If you memorize John 3:16, you will be able to tell them.

*Bible Verse:* "For God so loved the world, that he gave his only begotten Son, that whosoever believeth in him should not perish, but have everlasting life" (John 3:16).

*Prayer:* Dear God, thank you for loving us. Thank you for sending Jesus to live on earth and teach us about your love. Help us to tell people who don't know about you, that you love them too. Amen.

## Who's a Christian?

When two young men called at the Benson home, Faith listened to them when they asked Mother if they could tell her about their religion.

"No, thank you," Mrs. Benson said. "We are Christians. We do not believe as you do."

Later a pretty young girl and her mother came to call. They wanted Faith's mother to buy some pamphlets that explained their religion.

Again Mrs. Benson said, "No, thank you. We are Christians. We do not believe as you do."

"But we are Christians, too," the other woman answered.

Mother was quiet for a time. Then she said, "We believe Jesus is God's only begotten [born] Son. He was not just

33

a man; He was God in man. We believe He died for our sins. He rose from the grave. Someday He will come to take all who love Him to heaven. Then those who believe and trust in Him for their salvation will live with Him forever; those who do not love Him, will be separated from Him forever."

When the girl and her mother left, Faith said, "There are all kinds of religions, aren't there, Mother?"

"Yes, but there is only one *Christian religion.* All who believe in Christ and follow His teachings can be said to be Christians. As you grow older you will hear people say all religions are good. They will say, 'It doesn't make any difference what you believe just so you are sincere. The Hindus believe in God; the Muslims believe in God.' But remember, they don't believe in Jesus. Jesus said, 'I am the way, the truth, and the life; no man comes to the Father, but by me.'

"When you asked Jesus to forgive your sins and to come into your life, you became a Christian, Faith. You understand that, don't you?"

Faith nodded. "That's what my name means, doesn't it, Mother? *Faith,* faith in Jesus."

*Something to Think About:* Talk about the things that make the Christian religion different from other religions.

Read Matthew 16:13-18 where Jesus asks Peter to tell Him who he believes He is. Then notice what Jesus says about the true Christian Church.

*Bible Verse:* "Thou art Peter, and upon this rock [this faith that you have just claimed to believe] I will build my church; and the gates of hell won't be able to destroy it" (Matt. 16:18).

"There are some people who say with their lips that they believe in me [Jesus], but their hearts are far from me" (Matt. 15:8).

"If you confess with your mouth that you believe in

Jesus, and believe in your heart that God raised him from the dead, you shall be saved [become a part of the true Christian Church]" (Rom. 10:9).

*Prayer:* Dear Lord, thank you for giving us your Bible that tells us we must believe and trust you if we want to become members of the true Christian Church. But help us to love people who do not believe as we do. Help us to be such good Christians that they will want to learn more about your church. Amen.

## Let the Holy Spirit Fill You

"What does it mean to be filled with the Holy Spirit?" Kevin asked his father one day.

"First let's think about who the Holy Spirit is," Father answered. "He's God's Spirit, and He comes into our lives when we invite Him to. The Bible tells us we are Christians when the Spirit of God lives in our lives. To be filled with this Spirit means just that. There isn't room for badness in our life when we are filled with the Holy Spirit."

"I still don't understand," Kevin said.

"Come." Father led the way into the house. He found a piece of cloth. He soaked the cloth in oil so that it was filled with the oil. Then he dipped the oil-soaked cloth into a pan of water. Nothing happened. The cloth didn't soak up any of the water. It couldn't because it was too full of oil.

"There's no room for the water," Kevin said.

"Right. And a life filled with the Holy Spirit has no room for badness, either."

*Bible Verse:* "And I [God] will put my Spirit within you so you will live as I want you to and learn my commandments and do them" (Ezek. 36:27).

"The world cannot receive the Spirit because it doesn't know him, but you know him because he lives in you" (John 14:17).

"Realize that you are the temple of God, and that his Spirit lives in you" (1 Cor. 3:16).

"The Spirit lives in us; he tells us we are God's children" (Rom. 8:16).

*Prayer:* Dear God, thank you for giving us your Spirit to live in us, to teach us, and to keep us from sinning. Please fill our lives so full of your Spirit that there won't be any room for things that are wrong. Amen.

## "Lip" Christians

Cyretta Manford, Mother's college classmate, had just left after a short visit in the Applegren home.

Tommy Applegren felt he would never forget her visit.

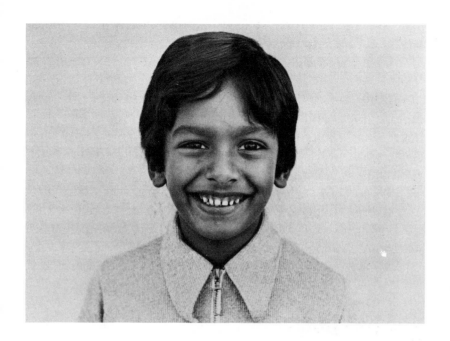

Cyretta was deaf, and he had never known a deaf person before. It was fun to talk to her because she could read his lips better than she could read his mother's or dad's.

From Cyretta Tommy learned that she didn't only watch his lips when he talked, she watched the expressions on his face and the movements of his hands and body, too.

She told Tommy a raised eyebrow, a sneer, a shrug of shoulders tells her as much about what a person is saying as his lips do.

"Once I was in a class where we were asked to read the lips of a person whose face was masked so only his lips showed," she told Tommy. "Then little by little the face was unmasked. And, to my surprise, the more of the face I saw, the better I read the lips."

*Something to Think About:* Can you tell whether a person loves Jesus by what he says?

Partly, but there is more to being a Christian than

just saying you are. Facial expressions, warm smiles, kindness—all help prove we love God.

Can you name other things that prove we belong to Jesus?

*Bible Verse:* "The people draw near to me with their mouth; they say they love me with their lips, but their heart is far from me" (Matt. 15:8).

"I will praise you, O Lord, with my whole heart [with all of me]" (Ps. 9:1).

*Prayer:* Dear Jesus, help us to be more than "lip" Christians. Help us to show by how we act and live that we belong to you. Help us to be kind and loving to those who are sick, lonely, or sad. Amen.

## Adopted Children

The Bible tells us that God had only one begotten (born) Son. When He sent Jesus to earth to be our Savior, He decided to send Him as a little baby. He chose Mary to be His boy's mother. When the angel Gabriel told Mary about God's plan she sang a song thanking God for choosing her to be the mother of Jesus.

Then the angel told Joseph about God's plan, too. When Joseph married Mary he really became Jesus' foster father. Joseph welcomed Jesus into his home. He loved Him and took good care of Him. But God was Jesus' real father.

When we become Christians we are adopted into God's family. The people who love and follow Jesus' teachings are our Christian brothers and sisters because they belong to the family of God too.

A song tells us what it means to belong to the family of God. The chorus begins, "I am so glad I'm a part of the family of God."

*Something to Think About:* Can you name some of your Christian brothers and sisters?

Are any of them sick? Are any in trouble? Have any had something good happen to them lately? Pray for those who have problems. Thank God because something good has happened to some members of the family of God.

*Bible Verse:* "Beloved, think how much God loves us [he sent his Son to us] so we can be called sons [children] of God" (1 John 3:1).

"Happy are they who put their trust in God" (Ps. 2:12).

*Prayer:* Dear God in heaven, thank you for sending Jesus to earth so we could learn to love Him and become your children. Amen.


## Tied Together in Love

Kim stepped out of the car and slammed the door hard, not knowing his twin brother's hand was in the way.

"Ohhhhh!" Ken cried. The pain was terrible. The door had squeezed several fingertips badly.

"I'm sorry," Kim told his brother. "I didn't mean to."

Ken held his hand tightly against his chest. Tears filled his eyes. "I know," he answered. "It's just that it hurts so much."

Mother took Ken to the doctor. There were no broken bones. The doctor bandaged the hand and told Ken to be careful with it until it healed. "It will be painful for many days," he said. To Ken it seemed to get worse as time passed. By now his whole hand hurt. Then his arm began to ache. By the time he went to bed he felt sick all over.

"It's funny," he told Kim. "One little part of my body hurts and I hurt all over."

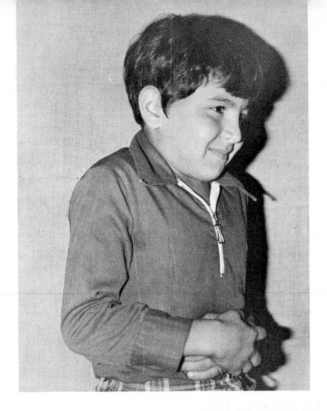

*Something to Think About:* Have you ever felt like Ken did? Then you will understand what we say about Christians being part of the family (the body) of Christ.

Each of us has some work to do in that body. It is as if you were the eye, someone else a hand, and someone a foot. When one part of the body of Christ hurts, all parts feel badly just as Ken's hand and arm did, and as his brother, Kim, did. If one member of Christ's body receives a reward or an honor, the rest of the body is glad this happened to a member of their body.

If one member is hungry or has some other need, other members are meant to help him. In Bible times, the Thessalonians sent food to the people in Jerusalem when they heard they were hungry.

Too, if one member sins, the rest of the body of Christ feels badly. They know that people will lose respect for the body of Christ (the church) when any member sins.

So you see, just as a family is tied together in love, the church, the body (the family) of Christ is tied together in love.

*Bible Verse:* "So we being many, are one body in Christ" (Rom. 12:5).

"If one member suffers, all members suffer; if one is honored, all rejoice" (1 Cor. 12:26).

Read 1 Corinthians 12:14-22 and verse 26.

*Prayer:* Dear Lord God, we love you because you are our heavenly father. Show us how to be good members of the body of Christ. Help us not to be jealous of other members. Help us to be quick to help those who are in trouble. Help us to rejoice and be glad when someone else earns an honor or a reward. Help us to understand what it means to be tied together in love. Amen.

## Are You Growing?

Aunt Elizabeth hadn't seen her nephew, Dennis, for several years. When she arrived from New York for a visit with the Bergren family, she clapped her hands the moment she saw Dennis.

"So this is Dennis!" she exclaimed. "My, how you have grown. Why, I remember when I was here last you were...," she measured a distance from the floor, "this high."

Dennis stiffened.

"Aren't you going to say hello to Aunt Elizabeth?" Mother asked.

"Hello, Aunt Elizabeth." As soon as the words were out of his mouth, Dennis turned to his mother. "May I go now?"

41

Mother nodded, but Dennis could see she wasn't pleased.

That night when Dennis had gone to bed, Mother visited his room. "You weren't very friendly when you greeted Aunt Elizabeth," Mrs. Bergren told her son. "Why?"

Dennis sighed. "That's all I ever hear when people come to visit. 'My how you have grown!' 'I remember when you got your first tooth,' or 'I remember when you learned to walk.' "

Mother chuckled. She gave Dennis a big hug. "Oh, Dennis, you're so funny. Aren't you glad you have grown? What if you hadn't? What if people said, 'What a little tyke. Aren't you ever going to grow up?' 'Hey, why don't you eat your spinach?' "

Now Dennis laughed. "I guess you're right, Mother. I never thought about it that way."

*Something to Think About:* To grow and mature physically is a wonderful thing. But to grow and become like Jesus is even more important.

Do you think that Aunt Elizabeth thought Dennis had grown and become more like Jesus since she last saw him?

Perhaps. We hope so.

The Bible tells us about people who didn't grow and become better Christians. They stayed babies in Christ.

You eat to make your body grow. What must you do to grow to be like Jesus?

*Bible Verse:* "But speaking the truth in love, we will grow up to be like him [Jesus]" (Eph. 4:15).

"Grow in spiritual strength and become better acquainted with our Lord and Savior Jesus Christ" (2 Pet. 3:18).

*Prayer:* Dear Jesus, we don't want to be baby Christians all of our lives. Help us to grow tall and strong in our love and faith just as we grow tall and strong physically.

Thank you for parents, pastors, and Sunday school teachers who help us learn to know you better. Amen.

## Buttons in Back

Lorrie wouldn't let anyone help her to do the things she believed she could do for herself. When she was a very small child, she learned to tie her own shoelaces. Shortly afterward she decided she didn't need anyone to help her get dressed. "I can do it," she told her family.

But one Sunday morning Lorrie had a problem. "Mother!" she called. "Please come and help me."

"I will, as soon as I finish washing the breakfast dishes," Mother answered. Lorrie couldn't wait. She ran into the kitchen.

Mother laughed. "You mean to say you can't get dressed by yourself?" she teased.

"Not with this dress," Lorrie answered. "I can't reach . . ." She stretched her hands behind her back. "See. The buttons are in back, but I'm in front."

*Something to Think About:* Mother thought this was a good time to talk to Lorrie about problems.

"Lorrie," she began, "as you grow older you will face many problems that are harder to handle than buttons on a dress. You'll dislike someone you should like—perhaps one of your teachers. You'll have to face sickness, sorrow, even the death of someone you love very much. You won't be able to handle all of these problems by yourself. That's when you will need the help of someone who is wiser than you are. Never be afraid to ask someone to help you with a problem you can't solve."

Mother was right. Everyone needs help at some time

or other. Though parents can often help, there will be times when you will need God's help more than anyone else's. Ask Him to help you just as Lorrie asked her mother to help her with the buttons on her dress.

*Bible Verse:* "God is a very present help in trouble" (Ps. 46:1).

"My help comes from the Lord who made heaven and earth" (Ps. 121:2).

*Prayer:* Dear Lord, we do get angry. Sometimes we are sad. Sometimes we wonder what we should be when we grow up. We are afraid when we are sick. We need you, Lord. We know you will help us because you care what happens to us. Amen.

## Do You Know What?

The Stellheimers are a fun-loving family. Of all the games they play together they like their "I-love-you" game the best. Sometimes Mr. Stellheimer says, "David, do you know what?"

David answers with a question of his own. "No, what?"

"I love you," his father tells him as he puts his arm around the boy's shoulder and hugs him.

"And I love you too," David tells his father as he returns the hug.

Sometimes Mrs. Stellheimer asks Mary, "Do you know what?"

"No, what?" Mary says.

"I love you."

"And I love you too, Mother." Mary quickly plants a kiss on her mother's cheek.

One day Mrs. Stellheimer was busy waxing the kitchen floor. Jerry, the youngest child in the family, rushed into the room. "Mother, do you know what?" he asked excitedly.

"What?"

"I love you."

"I love you too, Jerry," his mother answered as she continued waxing the floor.

Jerry asked the questions again. Mother played the game with him without once looking up from her work. When Jerry said, "I love you," his mother answered, "I love you too."

Jerry looked at his mother and waited. Finally he stamped his foot on the floor. "Well, why don't we do something about it then?" he asked.

*Something to Think About:* What do you think Jerry wanted his mother to do?

It's easy to say, "I love you," without showing the person we are talking to that we really do love him. But a hug or a kiss isn't the only way we can show members of our family that we love them. Can you name other ways we can prove our love?

Jesus told His followers, "If you love me, you will also obey me." So you see, being obedient proves love too.

*Bible Verse:* "Dear friends, because God loves us as much as He does surely we ought to love each other" (1 John 4:11).

*Prayer:* Dear Jesus. Thank you for your great love for us. We know we can prove our love to you if we obey you. Help us to obey you. Help us to obey our parents too so we can prove we really love them. Help us to be kind to our brothers and sisters. Keep us from quarreling and fighting. Be with us every minute during this day. Amen.

## You Are a Very Special Person

Carlos never grew tired of watching his father chip away at the block of white marble he had bought in Italy. "You may stay if you do not disturb me," his father told him. So whenever Carlos slipped into his father's studio, he did so quietly. He pulled up a stool a few feet from his father and sat with his elbows on his knees and his chin cupped in his hands, watching every motion he made.

Usually his father greeted him with a nod and a smile, then he returned to his work. Carefully measuring, turning, chipping, there were times when he forgot Carlos was there. On very special occasions he talked to Carlos and explained everything he did.

Weeks passed. Finally the bust (head and shoulders) of a man began to take shape. From then on Carlos' father worked far into the night long after the boy had gone to sleep.

One morning Carlos discovered a white cloth covered the bust his father had carved. "I have a surprise for you," the sculptor told his son. "Come." He led the boy to the statue. With a flourish he lifted the cloth and there in all its white marble splendor sat Abraham Lincoln.

Carlos gasped. He had never seen anything so beautiful. He turned to his father. "O Fa-th-ther," he stuttered. "How . . . how did you know he was in there?"

*Something to Think About:* Was Lincoln in the marble? Not at first. More likely he was in the mind and imagination of the sculptor. Then he was put in the marble.

Inside of you is a very special person, too. But you were in the mind of God first. Then He created *you* to be *you* and no one else. You are important to Him. He loves you. He has special work for you to do.

*Bible Verse:* "Before I formed you, I knew you; before you were born, I decided you should be a special person" (Jer. 1:5).

*Prayer:* Dear heavenly Father, there are times when we don't feel we are or can ever become very special persons. Please help us to realize we are important to you. Help us to understand what talents you have given us. Then help us to develop these talents for service for you. Amen.

## The Castle That Disappeared

A very old legend tells the story about a beautiful castle that sank into the ground very mysteriously. Many people believed the castle would rise again if lovely music were played at the spot where it disappeared.

Believing this rumor, musicians came from near and far to try to bring the castle back again. A shepherd played soft, lilting notes on his flute. A young woman strummed her harp. Some people sang; others chanted. But nothing happened. The castle remained in the ground.

Then one day a young boy came up with an idea he believed would make the castle reappear. "What would happen," he asked, "if all the musicians played and sang the same melody at the same time?"

"Let's try," the musicians said. A leader was chosen and when he gave the signal, musicians who had gathered from all over the world began to play and to sing the melody he had chosen.

It worked! The earth began to move. Little by little the castle pushed its way through the earth. People continued making music together. Before long the entire building rose from the ground. As magnificent as ever it glistened like gold in the bright sunlight.

*Something to Think About:* We know this is only a make-believe story. It tells us something, though. There are some things that can't be done by one person alone.

What would a church be like if only one person joined it? Can you imagine a choir with only one singer? And what about Sunday school? What would a hospital be like with only one nurse or doctor?

Now think about your home. Are there some things that are done better and more easily when two, three, or even four persons work together to do them?

*Bible Verse:* "May the God of steadfastness and encouragement help you to live in harmony [peace] with each other and in such unitedness [togetherness] with Christ, that together you will be like one voice glorifying the Father of our Lord Jesus Christ" (Rom. 15:5, 6).

"Two are better than one; they are rewarded by working together" (Eccles. 4:9).

*Prayer:* Dear Lord, you are the one who has taught us that it is good to work together. You placed the sun, the moon, and the stars in the sky to work together. We know we could not have rivers or lakes unless raindrops worked together to make them. All of your creation works together to glorify you. Help our family to work together to glorify you, too. Don't let any of us stop loving you. Help us, too, to share our time and talents with each other. Make our church a place where people love to work together in peace. Amen.

## Parking-Meter Kindness

One day Mr. Kidwell and his son, Jerry, went shopping. As Mr. Kidwell pulled up to the curb with his car, another car pulled up beside him. A woman in a big hurry got out of her car. She opened her purse and took out a nickel for the parking meter. But instead of putting it in her meter she put it in the one in front of Mr. Kidwell's car.

Quickly he unfastened his seat belt and opened his door to call to her. But by that time she was lost in a crowd of shoppers.

"Goody!" Jerry said. "Now you don't have to pay."

*Something to Think About:* What do you think Mr. Kidwell answered Jerry?

Can you quess what he did?

To Jerry's surprise he took out a nickel and dropped it in the parking meter in front of the woman's car.

Why do you think he did that?

*Bible Verse:* "Do to others as you would want them to do to you" (Luke 6:33).

"If you know what is right and don't do it, you sin" (James 4:17).

*Prayer:* Dear Lord Jesus, thank you for telling us that we should act toward others as we would want them to act toward us. Help us always to be honest and not try to cheat. Amen.

## More Money Than You Have!

"I'm richer than you are," Jay boasted one day after he and his sister, Paula, had counted the money in their piggy banks. "I've got more money than you have."

"I know," Paula answered. She acted as if she didn't care.

Jay put his money back in the bank and shook it in front of his sister. "More money," he teased. "I've got more money than you have. Don't you wish you had as much as I have?"

"I have all I need," Paula answered as she began to put her money back into her bank.

After Paula had left the room, Mother, who had heard Jay boast about his money, said, "That wasn't very nice, Son."

"Well, I do have more money than she has."

"Do you know why?" she asked. She reached for her coat. "Think about that while I go to the store."

*What did she mean?* Jay pondered after she had left. Why didn't Paula have as much money as he? Well, for one thing she spent it more often.

*For what?* Jay asked himself. He began to think of the ways Paula spent her money.

There was the time she gave a dollar to the missionary to help Korean orphans. And the time she paid for Sally Lou's school lunch because she had lost her money. Jay remembered, too, that Paula had bought Mother a pretty plant even though it wasn't her birthday. And the day the little neighbor boy dropped his ice-cream cone Paula bought him another one. And the time . . . .

No wonder she didn't have as much money as he. Thinking about it made him realize that Mother was right. He hadn't been very nice to Paula.

There was only one thing to do. He picked up his bank and headed for Paula's room. He knocked on her door. She opened it a crack. But when she saw Jay she hurried to close it. Jay was too quick for her. He put his foot in the opening.

"I'm sorry, Paula. I'm a stinker. Please forgive me?"

*Something to Think About:* Is it wrong to save money?

Was Jay really richer than Paula?

Why do you think Paula spent her money as she did?

Did she brag about what she had done?

How do you spend your money?

*Bible Verse:* "When you give, give generously, quietly, and in secret, for God who sees you in secret will reward you openly" (Matt. 6:3-4).

*Prayer:* Dear God, thank you for giving us the greatest gift of all, your Son Jesus Christ. When we give, help us to give cheerfully and generously to your work. When we help others, help us to be like Paula and do it quietly without boasting. Amen.

# How To Be Happy

Mr. Finney owns one of the few horse-shoeing places in the California county where Mark Douglas lives. Mark enjoys watching Mr. Finney put new shoes on the horses that customers bring to him. That's because Mr. Finney loves horses. He handles them gently, speaks to them softly. More important, he is the happiest man Mark has ever known.

"Mr. Finney, what makes you so happy?" Mark asked one day. "Dad said you never get mad."

"Can't say as I do. Not often, anyway." Mr. Finney answered. "I like people and seems they like me."

"Can I learn to be happy like you?"

"Reckon you can if you try."

"How?"

Mr. Finney put down his work. He folded his big arms across his chest. "Tell you what. You do three things for me and when you are through come back. Then I'll tell you how you can be happy like me.

"First find someone who is sick and bring him some fruit or flowers. Then find someone who is poor. Share. Give that person something that belongs to you. Something you know he will like. Now, the last thing, do something for someone who is old or who needs your help."

"I'll start right now," Mark told Mr. Finney as he jumped on his bike and rode away.

The first assignment was easy. Pastor Carlson's wife was sick. Mark asked his mother if he could pick some oranges and bring them to her. Mother thought that was an excellent idea.

Tears filled Mrs. Carlson's eyes when she thanked Mark for the oranges. "You have made me very happy," she said.

*Me, too,* Mark thought as he rode away.

What next? Someone who is poor. I know. Chip Parosky. Mark remembered the last time they had played catch together. Chip's mitt was old and torn. Mark thought about his own mitt. He'd had it for only a short time. Give that to Chip? He began to think how happy Chip would feel if someone gave him a new mitt. I'll do it.

Seeing Chip's face light up when he handed him the mitt made Mark ride away whistling a merry tune.

Now someone who is old. Widow Sanders? She always seemed so little and so tired and he had noticed that her lawn needed mowing. I'll help her.

He rang the door bell, but she didn't answer. Napping maybe. He tried knocking. Still no answer. Hard of hearing, he'd heard his mother say. Well, no matter. *I'll get her mower and cut her lawn while she sleeps,* he thought.

Mark pushed and pulled the old lawnmower back and forth through the long grass until he was so tired he could hardly move. Just when he had put the mower away, Mrs. Sanders opened her back door and stepped outside. Mark slipped behind a bush and watched her.

"Mercy me," she said aloud to herself. "One of the good Lord's angels, that's for sure!" The look of happiness and relief that spread across her face made Mark feel being tired was worth all the work.

Three things! He had done them all. And he'd never felt happier in his life. He hurried to tell Mr. Finney.

"So, you are back. Expecting me to tell you how to be happy, I reckon?" Mr. Finney asked in a teasing voice.

"Oh no, Mr. Finney. Now I know."

*Something to Think About:* What did Mark decide makes a person happy?

Can you think of three people you can help as he did?

*Bible Verse:* "Give and it shall be given to you; good measure, pressed down, and shaken together, and running over" (Luke 6:38).

"Happy is he who has mercy on the poor [who helps them]" (Prov. 14:21).

*Prayer:* Dear Father in heaven, thank you for teaching us what it means to help others. Now we understand that to be happy we must forget ourselves and think about other people's needs. Help us as a family to be kind to each other. Forgive us for the many times we bicker and quarrel. In Jesus' name, amen.

# Tommy Lives Forever

When his best friend, Tommy, died from leukemia (a blood cancer disease) the whole world fell apart for Gary Cameron. He couldn't eat. He didn't want to play. He only wanted to go off by himself and hide.

*Why?* he asked himself. *Why?* Tommy was one of the best friends he had. He never picked fights. He always shared.

One night Mr. Cameron found Gary sitting on the back step of his Dallas home staring into space. He sat down beside his son.

"I know it's tough, Gary," Mr. Cameron said.

"But, Daddy, why? Why? Tommy was no older than I am."

"I can't explain why," Gary's father answered. "This is one of the mysteries of life. It does seem strange that God lets some older persons who are very ill live on, then takes a young boy like Tommy away from us."

He cleared his throat. "You know how much Mother loves our rose garden. Yet she often picks just the buds insteads of roses that are in full bloom. That's because she likes the buds so much. Maybe God is like that."

"But I miss him so much," Gary told his dad.

"I know. But you must remember that Tommy loved Jesus. That means that you will see him again some day in heaven."

"But they buried him."

"Only his body. Gary, do you remember the time we saw that water beetle at the lake last summer?"

Gary remembered. The beetle sat sunning itself on a

rock near the shore. Then slowly, very slowly, its shell began to break open. Out came a dragonfly. It spread wings that looked like tiny rainbows in the bright sunlight. Then it flew off over the lake and disappeared, leaving its black shell behind.

"Just as the dragonfly took off across the lake, Tommy's spirit left its body behind. So Tommy isn't in the body that was buried. He's safe with Jesus now."

*Something to Think About:* Have you ever seen a butterfly come out of its cocoon? It does the same thing the dragonfly did. It leaves its old body behind, too, when it flies away.

What did Jesus prove to us when He rose from the grave and went to heaven?

*Bible Verse:* "Precious in the sight of the Lord is the death of those who love him" (Ps. 116:15).

"I am the resurrection and the life: one who believes in me, even though he dies, he will live again" (John 11:25).

*Prayer:* Dear God, thank you for letting your Son come to earth and die for us. Thank you for raising Him from the dead to show us that we, too, will live again when our time comes to die. Help us to live for you here so that we can live with you in heaven forever. Amen.

## Great Men Forgive

In her book *Amos Fortune*, Elizabeth Yates tells the story of a famous slave by that name. He worked hard and finally earned enough money to buy his freedom from the man who owned him. He settled in Jaffrey, New Hampshire, where he became a tanner (a person who makes leather out of animal skins). Though his daughter was allowed to go to public school, the children often made fun of her because she was black.

When Amos Fortune went to church, he wasn't allowed to sit with the white members. He had to sit in the balcony. And when the church celebrated Holy Communion (the Lord's Supper), he wasn't allowed to take part. But he never complained. He treated everyone kindly.

When Amos Fortune died, he left a will that gave part of his savings to the town school. A part of it went to the church he had attended, to buy . . . listen, to buy a beautiful silver communion service to be used to serve the Lord's Supper.

*Something to Think About:* Why didn't Amos Fortune get angry and quit attending church when they wouldn't let him sit with the white members?

Why did he give the communion service to the church?

Most people who are treated badly try to get even. They never forgive a wrong. But, like Jesus, this Christian tanner forgave those who were mean to him.

*Bible Verse:* "Love your enemies, do good to them who hate you. Pray for persons who are mean to you" (Matt. 5:44).

"Be kind to each other. Remember, just as the Lord forgave you, you must forgive others" (Eph. 4:32).

*Prayer:* Dear Jesus, it isn't easy to do what you did when you said, "Father, forgive them, for they don't know what they do." Help us to forgive our enemies and to love those who are mean to us. Amen.

## I Believe in Prayer

If transistors
Can snatch up songs
From out of the air
For us to hear. . . .

If TV screens
Can bring us news
At once
From far and near. . . .

Shouldn't we trust
Almighty God
To hear what we say
Each time we pray?

*Something to Think About:* Do you understand how it is possible to listen to people over the radio though they are hundreds of miles away?

Do you understand how a television program broadcast from Europe can be seen immediately in your own living room?

Even if you don't understand, you know these things

really do happen. Then, though you don't understand exactly how God hears our prayers, it shouldn't be hard to believe He does, should it?

*Bible Verse:* "I love the Lord because he has heard my voice and my prayers" (Ps. 116:1).

*Prayer:* Dear heavenly Father, we love you and worship you. We know you are almighty and that you do hear our prayers . . . no matter where we are or at what time of the day we pray to you. Thank you for listening to us when we talk to you. Amen.

## A Big God

A Sunday school teacher asked her class to write the words LOVE IS LIKE GOD on a piece of paper. A boy named Mike began to print the letters. His paper looked like this:

That's as far as he got. He asked the teacher for another piece of paper.

"What happened?" she asked.

"I didn't know God was so big," Mike answered.

*Something to Think About:* God is a big God because His love is big enough for the whole world.

Think of other words that describe Him (wonderful, ever-present, loving, helpful, mighty, good, fair, patient, kind).

*Bible Verse:* "God is mighty" (Job 36:5).
"God is King" (Ps. 47:7).
"God is holy" (Isa. 5:16).
"God is a living God" (1 Tim. 4:10).
"God is the creator of heaven and earth" (Gen. 1:1).
*Prayer:* Dear God, we thank you because you are a living God and not a god that someone has made. You hear us when we talk to you. You are a loving God. You are big enough to love all the people in the world. You are a holy God. You are everywhere. Thank you, God, for being such a great God. Amen.


## Without Spot or Wrinkle

"Don't, Patty, don't!" Mother became so excited she shouted when she saw Patty turn down a corner of the storybook she had been reading to her younger brother, Tom.

Puzzled, Patty looked up. "What did I do?" she asked.

"Look at the corner of that page," Mother said. "That's what you did."

"I only wanted to mark my place," Patty said.

"Then use a bookmark even if it's only a piece of paper," Mother told her.

Mother reached for the book. "Here, let me show you something," she said. She smoothed the corner Patty had turned down. "See that crease? Do you think it will ever come out?"

Patty didn't think so.

"And do you know what will happen to the corner after it has been folded for a long time?"

Patty thought she knew. The corner would tear.

"Now suppose you do this to many corners of your book. And suppose some other child takes the book from the library. He turns down other corners or pages to mark his place. Tell me, Patty, would you like to own such a book?"

Patty shook her head. "I'm sorry, Mother, I guess I just didn't realize what I was doing."

*Something to Think About:* Did you know that turning down a corner of a page of a book is like learning a new habit? When you do something that is wrong over and over again, what you think, say, or do makes such an impression or crease on your mind that it becomes a habit. When that happens you say, think, or do things without thinking. There's a verse in the Bible that says our lives should be without "spot or wrinkle." A wrinkle may be a crease in the corner of a book or a crease in our mind.

What is the best way to keep page corners from tearing?

What is the best way to keep from learning a bad habit?

*Bible Verse:* "Because you know these things, be careful so you don't do what you know is wrong and spoil your good intentions" (2 Pet. 3:17).

*Prayer:* Dear Jesus, please help us to live so that the words of our mouth, the thoughts of our minds, and all we do will be pleasing to you. Fill us with your love so that people will know that we belong to you. Amen.

## God Is Like a Mother

Jeffrey awakened with a start. He grabbed his throat. Then he let out a deep sigh. It was only a dream! He had thought someone was choking him. But no one was. It was just that his throat still hurt from his tonsil operation.

He wished he had a drink of water. But he knew if he went to get one he would disturb his mother, and he didn't want to do that. She was tired. She had spent one whole night with him at the hospital.

He lay down and pulled the covers over his shoulders.

A hand touched his forehead. It was Mother! "Would you like a drink of water?" she asked.

"How did you know?"

"Because I'm a mother."

*Something to Think About:* Mothers have a special sense that tells them when their children need something.

God is like a good mother. He knows all about us. Often He helps us before we even ask Him to.

*Bible Verse:* "Before they call, I will answer" (Isa. 65:24).

"For your Father [God] knows what things you need before you ask him" (Matt. 6:8).

*Prayer:* We feel like shouting, "Thank you, God!" You love us and take such good care of us. Often we forget that you do. You give us sleep at night. You heal our wounds. You make vegetables and fruit grow so we have food to eat. Thank you, Lord, for everything. Amen.

## Others

One Sunday after the minister had prayed the Lord's Prayer, "Our Father, who art in heaven. . . ," he read a poem. He said he didn't know who had written it.

> You cannot pray the Lord's Prayer
> And even once say *I*;
> You cannot pray the Lord's Prayer
> And even once say *my*.
>
> Nor can you pray the Lord's Prayer
> And then forget another.
> For when you ask for daily bread
> You must include your brother.
>
> For others are included
> In each and every plea.
> From beginning to the end of it
> It doesn't once say *me*.

Susan Brown and her two brothers, Mike and Charley, talked about this poem on the way home from church. They decided to study the Lord's Prayer to find out if what the poem said is true.

At home they took their Bibles and turned to Matthew 6 and read verses 9 through 13.

What do you suppose they learned?

*Something to Think About:* Now take your Bible and turn to Matthew 6:9-13. Can you find a single *I*? A *me*? Or a *my*?

Does this mean we should never pray for ourselves? Not at all. We need to pray for ourselves. But we must not forget to pray for others, too.

One Christmas the founder of the Salvation Army (a group of people who work with needy people) sent a greeting to all his workers around the world. This greeting contained just one word: OTHERS. General Booth, the leader of the group, wanted to remind these people that they must not think only of themselves but of others, too.

*Bible Verse:* "Admit your faults one to another, and pray for each other" (James 5:16).

*Prayer:* Dear Lord God, most of the time when we talk to you we say I, me, and my. Today we want to pray for others. Bless the nurses and doctors who take

care of sick people. Bless our mailman, our newspaper
boy, the men who pick up our trash. Help our missionaries
today. And please help the leaders of our country to do
what is right. Thank you for our minister and for our
Sunday school teachers. Thank you for relatives and friends.
Amen.


## God Got No Hands

---

A little boy named Sammy lived in a children's home
in Alaska with several other children and their housemother
and father.

All the children in the home owned Bibles. But because
Sammy had just come to the home, he didn't own one.
One day he went to Mamma (that's what the children
called their housemother) and said, "Can Sammy have
a Bible, too?"

"I am sure God has one for you. I will look and see,"
Mamma told Sammy.

Later she gave Sammy a Bible, one of many that had
been sent to her by Christian friends in the lower United
States.

Happy as could be, Sammy ran to show the Bible
to the rest of the children.

"See what God give me," he said, holding the Bible
high above his head.

The children examined the book. Then one of the boys
shook his head. "That's not your Bible. Your name not
in it."

"It is so mine. God gave it me."

"Then why not your name in front?"

Sammy thought for a while; then he said, "God got

no hands; he can no write my name."

*Something to Think About:* Sammy was right. God doesn't have hands like our hands. Listen to this story and see if you can tell why. After World War II when some soldiers in Germany began to rebuild a bombed church, they came across a broken statue of Jesus. They decided to put it together. They had a problem, though. They couldn't find the statue's hands. What should they do?

Finally one of the soldiers came up with an idea. He built a base for the statue of Jesus to stand on. Across the base he carved the words, CHRIST HAS NO HANDS BUT OUR HANDS.

Really the soldier was saying the same thing Sammy said. But he understood something Sammy didn't know. *People who love God are His hands.* They do things Jesus would do if He were here on earth.

Whose hands did God use to make it possible for Sammy to get a Bible?

*Bible Verse:* "Let your light so shine before men, that they will see your good works, and glorify your God in heaven" (Matt. 5:16).

"Because you do something for someone else in my [Jesus'] name, it is the same as doing it for me" (Matt. 25:40).

"For we are workers together with God" (1 Cor. 3:9).

*Prayer:* Dear Jesus, we love you. We thank you for the people who helped Sammy get a Bible. Show us how to be your hands and do the things you want us to do. Amen.

## "Whitey!"

Perry came up the walk dragging his sweater and baseball bat just as his father, Mr. Simpson, drove into the driveway.

"Something wrong?" Mr. Simpson asked as he stepped out of his car.

"It's Jason. I hate him."

"You do? Well, I wouldn't worry about that. God loves him, even if you don't."

"He couldn't . . . not a mean kid like that."

"What did he do?"

"He kicked me off the team."

"He must have had a reason."

Perry didn't answer.

"Speak up," his father told him.

"I called him 'Whitey.'"

"Perry!" Mr. Simpson dropped his briefcase and grabbed his son's shoulder. He shook him hard. "Don't ever let me hear you call anyone 'Whitey.' You don't like when someone calls you 'Blackie.'"

"That's what he did."

Mr. Simpson picked up his briefcase. "Then you are both at fault," he said. "Now go and clean up. I'll talk to you later."

Later Perry's dad called him into the kitchen. Perry was surprised to find Jason was there, too. "I asked him to come," Mr. Simpson said. "There's something I want to show you boys."

On the counter stood a pitcher full of lemonade. Beside the pitcher were two glasses, one brown and one white. Mr. Simpson took a teaspoon and let the boys taste the lemonade in the pitcher. Then he poured some of it into the glasses. He asked each boy to taste the lemonade in the glasses.

The boys did as they were told.

"Any difference?" Mr. Simpson asked.

The boys shook their heads. Then they looked at each other sheepishly. Finally they began to laugh. Jason turned to Perry's dad. "We understand, Mr. Simpson, we understand."

*Something to Think About*: Why do you think Mr. Simpson asked the boys to taste the lemonade in the glasses he had filled with lemonade that came from the pitcher? Did the color of the glasses change the taste? What did Perry and Jason come to understand?

Does a person's skin color change when he asks Jesus to come into his heart? What does change?

72

If you know the following little chorus, sing it together.

> Jesus loves the little children,
> All the children of the world;
> Red and yellow, black and white,
> All are precious in His sight.
> Jesus loves the little children of the world.

*Bible Verse:* "For God so loved the world, that he gave his only begotten Son, that *whosoever* believeth in him should not perish, but have eternal live" (John 3:16).

*Prayer:* Dear Lord God, we thank you for loving everyone. We thank you for sending your Son so that whoever wants to accept Him can live with you forever. Help us to love all people no matter who they are. Help us to be especially kind to those whose color is different from ours. Amen.


## Only Weeds

One summer Mr. Broder planted two gardens, one three times bigger than the other. He fertilized the large garden. He watered it when there was no rain. And with the help of his sons, Don and Jerry, he pulled every weed that pushed its way out of the ground.

But he never touched the small garden. He didn't fertilize it. The few vegetables that did come up were soon crushed by a splendid crop of weeds.

"Shouldn't we pull them too?" Don and Jerry asked their father one day.

"No, let them grow."

"But why?" the boys asked.

"Wait and see." The boys' father sounded very mysterious.

Some weeks later Don and Jerry heard their father talking to their next-door neighbor, Mr. Swelterman, in the garden. The two men were good friends even though Mr. Broder had never been able to get his neighbor interested in church. Mr. Swelterman always said no, he wasn't a church man. He didn't believe in sending his children to Sunday school, either.

"I wouldn't want to influence my children one way or the other," he said. "When they are old enough, they can choose what they want to do about religion."

Now in the garden, Mr. Broder pulled a plump yellow carrot out of the ground. He hosed off the soil and handed it to Mr. Swelterman who took a generous bite.

"Say, that's good," the man said. "This is some garden." He looked at the neat rows of vegetables. Then he spied the patch of ground that hadn't been cared for. He raised his eyebrows, a puzzled expression on his face. "What happened here?" he asked. "Certainly you don't call that weed patch a garden."

Mr. Broder rubbed his chin and smiled. "No, I guess not," he answered. "I just wanted to try an experiment. Right from the start I decided not to tell this patch of ground what to do. I let it choose for itself how to grow. And as you can see, it decided to grow weeds."

*Something to Think About:* What do you think Mr. Broder was trying to tell Mr. Swelterman?

Do you believe he understood?

Will children make the right choices when they are older if they are not taught to make them when they are young?

Who is supposed to help them?

*Bible Verse:* "Train up a child in the way he should go, then when he is older he will remember what he is taught" (Prov. 22:6).

*Prayer:* Lord God, we have learned how important

74

it is for us to begin going to Sunday school and church when we are young. We want to learn more about you. We want to learn how to pray and work for you. We want you to be our Savior. Amen.


## Play-Dough

It was one of those blustery evenings when rain poured out of the sky. Lightning flashed. Thunder roared like an angry lion.

"Do we have to go to bed?" six-year-old Melinda Barkman asked. "Can't we stay up until the storm stops?"

"I suppose you can," Mother answered. "You wouldn't be able to go to sleep now, anyway. Perhaps we should play a game together."

"Play-dough! I want play-dough!" Melinda cried.

Mother raised questioning eyebrows as she looked at Bart and Susan, the two older Barkman children. "Okay?" she asked as she winked at them.

"Okay," they answered.

While Melinda ran to get the play-dough, Daddy, Mother, Bart, and Susan pulled up chairs around the dining room table. Soon everyone was busy working with a ball of clay Mother gave to them.

No one talked for a long time. Instead they thumped, twisted, and pulled their clay. Melinda began to make a doll. Then she changed her mind and began to make a cat.

"Mommy, look!" she cried excitedly. "I can do anything I want to with the play-dough."

"You can?"

"Yup. It just lets me."

*Something to Think About:* Play-dough is a lot like the clay that a potter uses to make pots and vases or a sculptor uses to make statues.

Did you know that the Bible talks about clay? It says that God is the potter and we who belong to Him are the clay.

Remember what Melinda said about her play-dough? "It just lets me do anything I want to with it."

Does this mean anything to you when you think of yourself as God's clay which He shapes to make what He wants you to be?

*Bible Verse:* "Behold, as the clay is in the potter's hand, so are you in my [God's] hand" (Jer. 18:6).

*Prayer:* Dear Lord, because you are the potter, we know you have a plan for our lives. Show us what that plan is. Make us into the kind of people you want us to be. Amen.

## Take Care!

At church the Jones family sang the song, "This is my Father's world. . . ." They listened to the pastor talk about the world God made: the sun and moon, the stars, animals, birds, trees, flowers, and fish of the sea.

Later at home they talked about the Pastor's sermon. Sally asked, "Does this mean that everything in the world belongs to God?"

"He made everything," Mr. Jones answered.

"We just borrow it, don't we?" Sammy, Sally's twin brother, wanted to know.

"Of course," Sally answered. "And we can keep it as long as we like."

"I'm not so sure about that," Mr. Jones answered. "It all depends."

"On what?" Sammy asked.

"On how well we take care of it."

*Something to Think About:* Taking care of God's world is important to all people. Today everyone is talking about how we should take care of the world God has made. When God said man should have dominion (rule) over His world, He meant we should protect and take care of it. If we don't, it won't last as long as it should.

Let's try an experiment. Listen to the following statements. Say *yes* if you believe good care is being practiced. Say *no* if you believe the sentence describes bad care of God's world.

1. A boy buys a candy bar. He unwraps it and throws the wrapper on his neighbor's lawn.

2. Dad, Mother, Bill, and Dave have been camping.

They put out their campfire and pour water over it to make sure that it won't spread and burn nearby trees.

3. A hunter kills birds just for the fun of it.

4. A woman goes to the store to buy an expensive leopard coat. It is expensive because it is made from the fur of an animal that is becoming more and more scarce.

5. A lumberman plants small trees where he has cut down big ones.

6. A family dumps garbage in a nearby lake.

What can you do to help take care of God's world?

*Bible Verse:* "The earth is the Lord's and all its fulness; the world, and all that lives in it" (Ps. 24:1).

*Prayer:* We thank you, dear God, for making a world with beautiful flowers and trees, and clean lakes and streams. We thank you for the animals you have created. We thank you for coal, oil, and salt you have put into the ground for our use. Help us not to waste these things. Help us to take good care of your world. Amen.

## Money for Shoes

Mrs. Rigmark taught in a Bible school in Japan. She was surprised one day when a girl who worked in her home to earn money to go to school came to see her.

"Would you give me some more work to do?" the girl asked.

"Why would you want more work?" Mrs. Rigmark asked.

The girl bowed her head. "To earn money for something I need," she whispered.

Mrs. Rigmark wondered what that could be, though she didn't ask the girl. But she did give her more work to do.

The night after the girl had been paid, Mrs. Rigmark saw her slip into the boy's section of the dormitory. She followed the girl, who went directly to the shelf where the boys placed their shoes each night. She slipped the money into a pair of shoes that belonged to a boy who needed a new pair very badly. Quietly she tiptoed back to her room. When she saw that Mrs. Rigmark had been watching, she put her finger over her lips warning her not to tell anyone.

The next morning the boy who had received the money wanted to know who had given it to him. The girl never said a word. Mrs. Rigmark didn't either.

*Something to Think About:* Think of something you can do for someone. Don't tell anyone what you do. Promise?

*Bible Verse:* "Be kind to each other, especially to those who love Jesus as you do" (Rom. 12:10).

"Love is kind . . . it doesn't brag about what it does" (1 Cor. 13:4).

*Prayer:* Dear God, thank you for the gift of your Son who was kind to all people. Help us to think of someone we can help today. Amen.

## Look Alikes

"Here they are," Elizabeth, who had been watching from the living-room window, called to her mother. "Daddy and Uncle Jim are here. They just drove into the driveway."

Clapping her hands excitedly, Elizabeth joined her mother as she went to the door. She was eager to see Uncle Jim again. She had been so small when he joined the Navy she hardly remembered him at all. But she still had the Raggedy Anne doll he gave her before he left.

The door burst open. Uncle Jim took Mother into his arms and hugged her. He knelt beside Elizabeth, took her hand and kissed it.

"So this is the little girl I left behind" he said. "I hope we'll be great friends."

Elizabeth hoped so, too. While they ate dinner Uncle Jim asked Elizabeth about her school. He asked her about her pets and about her friends.

Suddenly he turned to Mother. "You know, Judy," he said, "this girl is so much like you I'm sure I would have known her anywhere. She talks like you. She tosses her head the way you do. And when she smiles her eyes smile too, just as yours do."

Elizabeth was glad Uncle Jim thought she talked and smiled like her mother. She wanted to be like her mother in other ways, too. Mother never yelled when she scolded. Sometimes Elizabeth yelled when she became angry.

And when Mother played the organ at church services, Elizabeth liked to close her eyes and pretend she was flying through the air on a magic carpet with music floating all around. Elizabeth hoped she would be able to play the organ as well as her mother someday.

*Something to Think About:* Why do you think Elizabeth talked and laughed like her mother?

What must Elizabeth do to learn to play the organ as well as her mother?

It's good that Elizabeth wanted to be like her mother. It's important, too, for her to want to be like Jesus. Jesus loved all people—tax collectors, lepers, sinners, mothers and fathers, little children. He forgave people who were mean to Him.

How can Elizabeth learn to be like Jesus?

*Bible Verse:* "For I [Jesus] have given you an example that you should do as I have done" (John 13:15).

*Prayer:* Dear Jesus, help us to study the Bible so we can learn to live as you lived. Then help us to be like you. Help us to love all people and to forgive those who sometimes act as if they don't love you at all. Amen.


## We Show We Are Christians When We Pray

Uncle Jim liked to tell stories about his life in the Navy. One day he told Mother and Daddy about a Bible study he had taught on his Navy ship.

"How did you get started?" Daddy asked. "How did you know which fellows would be interested in a Bible study class?"

"It was this way," Uncle Jim answered. "When I first went into the Navy I missed my Christian friends. I didn't know how I could learn to know which men were Christians. Then I had an idea. At mealtime, before I bowed my head and thanked God for my food, I looked around to see if there were others who bowed their heads and thanked God for their food. Usually I found someone. After the meal I would hurry up to this person. 'Say, you are a Christian, aren't you?' I would ask.

"Most of the time the men would answer with a question of their own, 'How did you know?' I told them.

"In a short time I made several Christian friends. We began studying the Bible together. Soon other sailors joined us."

*Something to Think About:* The Bible tells us that before Jesus ate He broke bread, blessed it, and thanked God for it. His disciples did this too.

If you had been a sailor on Uncle Jim's ship, would he have thought you were a Christian?

*Bible Verse:* "In everything give thanks, for this is the will of God in Christ Jesus for you" (1 Thess. 5:18).

*Prayer:* Dear Jesus, thank you for our home. Thank you for the clothes we wear. Thank you for the food we eat. Help us never to forget to be thankful for all your goodness to us. Amen.

## I Want to Sing!

Amy Ludlow managed to hide her feelings as long as she was in Sunday school and church. But the moment the family car pulled out of the church parking lot, she buried her head in her mother's lap and burst into tears.

"What's with you?" Amy's brother, Kerby, asked.

"Shhhh!" Mother put her finger over her lips. "She'll tell us when she's ready."

Amy sat up. "It's teacher."

"Oh?" Father said. "And what did she do?"

"She asked Sally Jones to sing the welcome song at the Christmas program."

"I can understand that," Mother said. "Sally has a lovely voice."

"But I wanted to sing it."

"You mean croak it," Kerby teased.

"Kerby! That's enough," Father said. "Tell us, Amy, what did your teacher ask you to do?"

"I'm supposed to learn this long poem." She dug around in her purse until she found it. Then she handed it to her mother.

Mother read the poem slowly. "How nice, Amy. But it's quite long. Do you think you can memorize all of it?"

Amy nodded. "Teacher said I memorize things and remember them better than anyone in the class."

"Then what are you griping about?" Kerby asked. "I wish I could remember things like that."

Father began to laugh. "Now you sound like Amy did awhile ago. You both want to do what someone else does better than you. Why don't you thank God for what you can do?"

*Something to Think About:* Listen and talk about this poem written by poet Raply Seager.°

> I cannot sing another's song,
> For him so right, for me so wrong;
> I'll make my own come clear and fine.
> The chances are he can't sing mine.

*Bible Verse:* "Don't neglect [fail to develop] the gift God has given you" (1 Tim. 4:14).

"We shouldn't seek honors and popularity . . . nor should we be jealous of others" (Gal. 5:26).

*Prayer:* Dear Jesus, help us to understand and appreciate the talents you have given us. Help us to develop them. Help us not to be jealous of others who can do things we can't do as well. Amen.

---

° Used by permission of author.

## Gramps' Offering

The Tozer family awakened one Sunday morning to find that a bad blizzard had closed all of the roads.

"What will we do about church?" Eric asked his father.

"There's no church on Saturdays, Son," Gramps answered quickly.

"But, Gramps, today isn't Satur...," Jane, Eric's sister, began. She stopped when she saw her mother put a finger against her lips. Jane understood. Mother had told her children not to argue when Gramps differed with them. Gramps was growing more and more forgetful. Why, just the day before he had come into the kitchen right after he had eaten breakfast. He wanted to know when dinner would be ready.

"We'll have church right here," Charles Tozer, the children's father, told his family. At eleven o'clock they pulled up some chairs and sat down to watch a televised church service being broadcast from a nearby city. The family, even Gramps, joined the members of the congregation when they sang the hymns of worship. They bowed their heads and were very quiet when the minister prayed.

But when he made the church announcements, Gramps became restless. He put his hand in one pocket, then in another. "What do you know?" he muttered to himself. "Left my wallet at home." He turned to his son and whispered, "Loan me a five, Charles?"

Father took out his billfold and handed Gramps a five dollar bill. At the same time he whispered something in Eric's ear. The boy tiptoed into the kitchen. He returned with a small basket Mrs. Tozer used to serve bread at mealtime.

Father gave Jane some coins and slipped Eric a dollar bill. Then while the organist played the offertory, Eric passed the collection basket. Gramps smiled happily as he dropped his five-dollar bill into it. Everyone rose and sang the doxology, "Praise God. . . ."

From the corner of her eye, Jane saw her mother wipe tears from her eyes. Later she asked, "How come? How could Gramps remember the offering when he forgets so many other things?"

"Habit," Mrs. Tozer answered. "But what a wonderful habit!"

*Something to Think About:* You have learned that doing something bad over and over again can become a habit. Now you learn that doing something good over and over again can become a habit too.

The Bible says all Christians should give a tenth of what they earn to the Lord (that for children should include allowances). Many Christians give a great deal more. They believe that the more they have the more they should give to God. The Bible says that not giving is the same as stealing from God.

*Bible Verse:* "Everyone should give as he is able, according to the way God has blessed him" (Deut. 16:17).

*Prayer:* Dear God, thank you for the lesson that Gramps taught us. Help us each week to give back to you a part of what you have given to us. Help us to make giving a habit as Gramps did. In Jesus' name, amen.

## Jesus Talked to Peter Alone

Jesus met with many of His followers between the time He was raised from the dead and the time He ascended into heaven. Sometimes He talked to people in groups. At other times He talked to them alone.

After a lakeshore breakfast Jesus had prepared for His disciples, He talked to Peter alone.

"Simon Peter," He said, "do you love me more than you love your friends?"

"Yes, Jesus," Peter said. "You are my best friend."

Jesus questioned Peter again. "Do you really love me, Peter?"

"Yes, I really love you."

A third time Jesus asked, "Peter, are you sure you love me?"

Peter answered, "You know my heart. You know how much I love you."

*Something to Think About:* Jesus didn't ask Peter if he was rich. Nor did he ask him how much education he had. The color of his skin didn't matter to Jesus. He didn't care whether Peter wore fancy clothing or not. He only wanted to know if Peter really loved Him.

Jesus asks you the same question: "Do you love me?" Sooner or later you must answer it. Can you, like Peter, say, "Yes, Jesus, I really do love you"?

Now notice something else. When Jesus was sure that Peter loved him, He gave him work to do. He said, "Feed my sheep; feed my lambs." He knew Peter would make a good shepherd (leader). He wanted him to take good care of his flock (followers of Jesus). He knew he would teach them and help them.

If you tell Jesus you love Him, He will give you work to do, too.

Talk about the things you would like to do for Jesus.

*Bible Verse:* "I will delight [be glad] to do thy will, O my Lord. . ." (Ps. 40:8).

"Therefore, my beloved, be steadfast [dependable] unmoveable [faithful], always doing all the work you can for the Lord, for he knows what you do" (1 Cor. 15:58).

*Prayer:* Dear Lord God, we have read in the Bible that you have given each one of us a special talent to use for you. Help us to understand exactly what that talent is. Then make us willing to do what you want us to do. In Jesus' name, amen.


## Katie Kite

Katie Kite spread her wide wings in the air. She dipped to the right, then to the left. Suddenly she began to race with the wind. On the ground below, her owner, a tall, slender boy of twelve, raced with her across a grassy hill. Always in control, he kept a tight grip on the string that held her in the air.

*This is fun,* Katie thought. *But I want to go higher, higher!* She looked down at the string that kept her in tow. *If I had teeth I'd bite it in two, that's what I would do,* she told herself.

For a moment it seems as if the boy understood what Katie was thinking. He let out another length of string. Katie flew higher. Then she felt a tug. The string tightened again. It held her fast.

But not for long. A strong gust of wind picked Katie up and twirled her around and around. It crept under her and pushed her up . . . up . . . up. Then with one fierce blow it snatched the string out of the boy's hand.

Katie laughed and laughed. "I'm free, free!" she shouted. What fun. Now another run. Up, up, up! Katie could hardly see her owner now. He was like a clothespin on the ground.

The wind pushed Katie still higher. Then suddenly it went wild. It shoved Katie; then it pulled her down. Up, down, around and around. Frightened now, she raised her voice and shouted, "Pull me in; pull me in!" But the boy couldn't pull her in. He no longer held the string tightly in his hands. It dangled in the air.

When Katie was quite dizzy from all the tumbling and tossing, the wind grew tired of playing, and disappeared. And Katie Kite? She landed, ribs broken, in a garbage dump on the edge of town.

*Something to Think About:* We call this kind of story an *allegory* because it is a pretend story that teaches us a lesson. Can you tell what this lesson is?

Why is it important that a kite's owner keep a tight grip on a kite's string? Think about the kite and tell what happens to children when they are allowed to do anything they please.

Who should hold the string of their lives?

Do you sometimes wish you didn't have to obey your parents? Do you sometimes wish they would let you do as you please? If you do, remember Katie Kite.

*Bible Verse:* "Honor [love and obey] your father and mother; then you will be blessed with long life" (Ex. 20:12).

*Prayer:* Dear Jesus. Thank you for obeying your Father and doing what He wanted you to do when you lived on earth. Help all of us as members of this family to remember that no one is free to live as he pleases. Each of us must live by rules and regulations. Teach us to know what they are. Help us today to obey persons who hold the string of our lives. Help us to obey you too. Amen.

## Don't Be a People Weed

A little seed was planted in good soil. Watered by gentle rain, it began to sprout. *I wonder,* the little seed thought, *which of all the flowers should I decide to be?* It couldn't make up its mind.

It watched the lily push its way up through the ground to stand straight and tall beside the garden wall. It watched a rose bud and bloom.

"I don't want to be a lily," the little seed said. "It's too proud. I don't want to be a rose either. Its stems have thorns. A violet? A violet is too small and grows too close to the ground."

And so criticizing each and every plant, the little seed never tried to grow. Then one day it awakened to find it was too late to choose what it wanted to be. It had become as useless as a weed.

*Something to Think About:* There are men and women today who, when they were young, criticized everyone and everything. They wasted their lives. Now when they are old they find they, too, have become as useless as weeds.

Someday God is going to ask you what you have done with your life. What would you like to be able to tell Him?

*Bible Verse:* "So every man shall give account of himself to God" (Rom. 4:12).

"Walk wisely with others, redeeming [making good use of] the time" (Col. 4:5).

*Prayer:* Dear God in heaven, we know you want us to be what you planned us to be. You want us to grow and mature as good Christians should. Help us choose the work we are best suited for. Make us useful, not useless, persons. Amen.

## The Knitting Mistake

Tim listened to Grandmother's knitting needles make click-click noises as they moved in her hands. *How can she knit so fast?* he thought.

He moved closer so he could touch the soft red wool of the afghan that lay in Grandmother's lap. Suddenly his hand stopped. "Grandmother, look!" he cried as he pointed to a small hole in the afghan.

Grandmother looked. "Oh, my," she said. "I must have dropped a stitch." She put her needles down and began to rip the afghan.

Tim grabbed her hands. "Don't. You'll spoil it."

Grandmother smiled. "No, Tim, I won't spoil it. I would if I didn't go back to the place where I made the mistake.

I have to do that and then start again. If I didn't, I would always be sorry."

*Something to Think About:* It isn't only in knitting that we must go back to the place where we made a mistake and start again.

Suppose you said something that hurt someone badly. You could do two things. You could say, "So what?" and then forget all about it. Or you could go to that person and say, "Please forgive me." Which would be the right thing to do?

The Bible tells a story about a tax collector named Zacchaeus. When Jesus forgave his sins, he decided to go to the people from whom he had collected too much money and return four times what he had taken.

A boy took things from a store. When he learned to know Jesus he went to the owner and out of his allowance paid for the things he had taken.

*Bible Verse:* "If you lie, or do wrong, you must make it right, for God knows what you do" (Lev. 6:2-5).

*Prayer:* Dear Father in heaven, you are a good God. You love what is right; you hate what is wrong. Help us to remember things we have done that are wrong. Help us to make them right. Help us to be kind, helpful, honest, and fair. In Jesus' name, amen.

## I Thinks So

Karen was a very precocious child. This means she was very smart for her age. She walked when she was nine months old. When she was two she spoke as well as many four-year-olds. She seemed to understand things that much older children didn't understand.

One day she, Dad, and Mother went shopping in a store that had just opened for business. On one floor near the escalator stood a bouquet of beautiful artificial flowers.

Karen walked over to the flowers. Examining them, she cocked her head to one side, then to the other.

"Flowers . . . ," she said. She stepped closer and smelled the flowers. A puzzled look spread across her face. Then she turned to her parents, "I thinks," she added.

*Something to Think About:* Why did Karen say, "I thinks"?

Little as she was, she realized they weren't real flowers. How did she know this?

Someone has called artificial flowers *hypocrite* flowers. A hypocrite is someone who tries to be somebody he isn't. A hypocrite Christian may pretend he loves Jesus. He may go to church. He may sing in the choir. But unless he has given his life to Jesus, he is like the artificial flowers; he is an artificial Christian.

What about you? Have you ever asked Jesus to come into your life? If you haven't, you can ask Him right now.

*Bible Verse:* "But as many as believed in Jesus and received him, to them gave he power to become the sons of God [Christians]" (John 1:12).

*Prayer:* Dear Lord Jesus, I want to be a real Christian. I do not want to be an artificial Christian. I want to give my life to you so that someday I can live in heaven with you forever. Please forgive my sins and come into my life right now. Amen.

## Say "Please"

Mr. and Mrs. Brewster were called East to settle some business matters. While they were gone they left their son, ten-year-old Leland, in California with friends.

In the East, Leland's parents were surprised, though very pleased, to get reports about his good manners.

Their first dinner at home, however, was very disappointing. Leland gobbled his food. He talked with his mouth full. He refused to try the new dessert his mother had made. And he didn't once say *please* or *thank you.*

"Son," his father said, "I can't understand this. What have you done with the good manners the Morgans wrote about?"

Leland looked up, startled. "Goodness, Dad," he sputtered, "you don't think I act like this when I'm with *people?*"

*Something to Think About:* A framed motto that hangs in many homes says: HOME IS THE PLACE WHERE WE ARE TREATED THE BEST AND BEHAVE THE WORST.

Is this true? Should it be?

Should we treat others better than we treat those we love best?

How can we learn to practice good manners wherever we are?

You might try this little game. Put an empty bowl on the table. When any member of the family forgets to say *please* or *thank you* at meals, ask him to put a penny in the bowl. At the end of each week add the money to your Sunday school collection.

*Bible Verse:* "Try to agree with each other; be kind to each other, loving, understanding and *courteous*" (1 Pet. 3:8).

*Prayer:* Dear Jesus, help us to remember we are never alone even in our own homes. You are with us. You see how we act and speak. Help us to be kind and courteous to members of our own family as well as to others. Amen.

## Lips Speak, Ears Hear, Eyes See

Ricky gobbled his breakfast and sat fidgeting while he waited for his parents to finish eating their food. When his dad had taken the last bite of his waffle, Ricky handed him the Bible and the family devotional book. "Can we have devotions right now?" he asked.

"What's your hurry?" Father asked. "Going somewhere?"

"If Mom will let me," Ricky answered. "Gale's mother is having a garage sale, and people start coming real early. . . . I can go, can't I, Mom?"

"Do you have any money?"

"A couple of quarters. Just in case. But I don't think I'll spend them. I just want to see what Mrs. Brown is selling."

"You may go," Mother told Ricky. "Be back in an hour, though. I want you to go to the store for me."

Ricky went to the garage sale. And in an hour he was back. "Look what I bought," he said to his mother. "It cost a quarter." He held up a small statue of three monkeys. They sat close together on a small stand. One monkey covered his eyes with his paws. Another covered his ears with his paws. The third monkey's paws were crossed over his mouth.

Mother laughed when she saw the statue. "Those monkeys are acting out a wise Chinese proverb," she told Ricky. She pointed to the monkey whose paws covered his eyes. "See no evil," she said. She pointed to the monkey whose paws covered his ears. "Hear no evil." Then pointing to the monkey whose paws were crossed over his mouth, she said, "Speak no evil."

"I think you made a good investment, Ricky. If you remember what these monkeys tell you, you aren't likely to get into trouble."

*Something to Think About:* The dictionary tells us that the word *evil* means "bad." We all know there are television programs, movies, books, and magazines which are bad. To look at them would only do us harm, for what we see we put in our minds. A mind that is evil doesn't please God. How can we keep from seeing what is bad?

How can we keep from hearing what is evil?

When does a person speak evil?

*Bible Verse:* "Let the words of my mouth, and the thoughts of my mind be pleasing to you, O Lord, my strength, and my redeemer" (Ps. 19:14).

"If a man speaks no evil, he is a perfect man; he is able to control his whole body" (James 3:2).

*Prayer:* Dear heavenly Father, thank you for ears that can hear. Thank you for eyes that can see. Thank you for lips and a tongue that can speak. Help us to use these gifts for good and not for evil. Help us to see, hear, and speak only what you would want us to. In Jesus' name, amen.

# Spoiled or Spanked?

"Hello, Grouchy!" Mary greeted her little neighbor friend one day. Pouting, Borden sat on the street curb, a ball in his hand, his dog, Duke, at his side.

"I'm mad."

"Who are you mad at?"

"My mother," Borden answered glumly.

"What did she do?"

"She spanked me. I ran into the street after my ball without looking to see if a car was coming . . . and there wasn't any car coming!"

"What if there had been one?"

Borden didn't answer. Instead, he began to bounce his ball. Duke was playing with him. He tried to snatch it away from Borden. He missed. The ball rolled into the street. Duke tore after it just as a car rounded the corner. Tires screeched! When the car finally came to a stop, it was just inches away from Duke. Borden ran to get him. The driver looked like a mad bull. "Keep that dog off the street!" he yelled as he drove off.

When Borden reached the curb he shook Duke hard. Then he gave him the worse thrashing he had ever had.

"What did you do that for?" Mary asked.

"Because he didn't mind."

Mary looked at Borden. She pressed her lips together in a smirk. "I see," she said.

Borden did too. And now he understood. He wasn't mad at his mother anymore.

*Something to Think About:* Do you believe Borden's mother should have punished him? Why?

Why was Borden angry in the beginning and not at the end of the story?

*Bible Verse:* "He who doesn't punish his child when he does wrong doesn't care very much about him. He who loves his son punishes him" (Prov. 13:24).

*Prayer:* Dear Jesus, we are like Borden a lot of times. We get mad when our parents punish us for doing wrong. Forgive us. Now we understand that they punish us because they love us and want us to learn to do what is right. Help us to obey our parents. Amen.

## What Is Work?

Juan and Marcos were burned badly when their mobile home caught fire. Marcos had to have several skin-graft operations. These are operations where skin is taken from one part of the body and placed on another part to help it heal.

Since the boys' parents worked in the harvest fields, they coudn't take their boys to the doctor. Nor could they visit them in the hospital very often.

A kind missionary who worked with these Spanish-speaking people helped this family. She took the boys to the doctor. And day after day for several months she drove many miles to visit them in the hospital. On Sunday she held meetings for the parents who worked in the harvest fields. She taught Sunday school. And she helped other families who had special needs, too. Often she became very tired.

One day when the missionary was taking Marcos to the city for his checkup, he asked, "Miss Missionary, did you ever go to college?"

"I surely did . . . for five years. Why do you ask, Marcos?"

"Oh, I was just wondering. How come you never work?"

*Something to Think About:* What do you think of Marcos' question?

Do missionaries work? How?

Some people think missionaries and ministers work only during the hours they preach or teach. They forget these people work when they study and prepare sermons and Sunday school lessons. They work when they visit people in the hospital. They work when they visit and help people in their homes.

Many people work only eight hours or less a day. Sometimes Miss Missionary works as many as twelve hours a day. Someday ask your pastor to tell you about his work.

*Bible Verse:* "Whosoever calls upon the Lord shall be saved. But how can they call upon him if they don't believe? How can they believe unless they hear? And how can they hear without a preacher . . . ? How beautiful are the feet of people who preach the good news about Jesus Christ" (Rom. 10:14).

*Prayer:* Dear Lord Jesus, thank you for men and women who care about people's souls. Thank you for our minister and our missionaries. Please give them good health and keep them strong so they can do the work they are supposed to do for you. If you want someone in our family to be a minister and missionary, help that person to be willing to become what you want him (or her) to be. Amen.

## Let God Be Your Father

Cheryl's little friend, Mary Lou, often visited the Anderson home. Mother noticed that Mary Lou always talked about her mother but never talked about her father.

One day when the Andersons were riding to the beach Mother asked, "Cheryl, doesn't Mary Lou have a father?"

"No," Cheryl's older sister, Dana, answered quickly. "Her mother is divorced."

Cheryl poked Dana hard. "She does too have a father. God is her Father. So there!"

*Something to Think About:* Good for Cheryl! Don't you agree?

It would be wonderful if all children who don't have a father in their home could understand what Cheryl said.

If you don't have a daddy in your home, remember God is your Father. You can tell Him all your secrets. He listens to you because He loves you.

*Bible Verse:* "God is a father of those who don't have fathers" (Ps. 68:5)

"When you talk to God pray: Our Father, who art in heaven" (Matt. 6:9).

*Prayer:* God, we thank you that you are our Father. We thank you that you are the father of those who don't have fathers. You love us and want us to love you. We thank you that we can tell you all our secrets. We can tell you when we are afraid. You will be with us when we are lonely and when we are sick. Thank you, God, our Father. Amen.

## A Remembrance

Jane and Paul were sad. Grandmother was very ill and the doctor said she had only a short time to live. The children knew Jesus would take Grandmother to heaven when she died because she loved Him. But they would be lonesome for her just the same.

One day Grandmother called Jane and Paul into her bedroom. "I want to give you something," she said. "Here." She handed Jane a lovely china cup and saucer with tiny violets painted on them. "These belonged to my mother," she said. "Everytime you use them, remember that I loved you just as Jesus does."

She gave Paul a small silver compass. "This will keep you from getting lost when you go hiking," she said. "Everytime you use it remember that God is like a compass. He will keep you from being lost in your walk with Him."

"Thank you, Grandmother," Paul said.

"Thank you, Grandmother," Jane said. By now both children were close to tears.

"Now, now, don't be sad," Grandmother said. "I'm glad I am going to be with Jesus. Always remember that. I gave you the cup and saucer and the compass to help you remember me and to remind you to live so that you could meet me in heaven some day. Understand?"

*Something to Think About:* Did you know that Jesus gave us something to remember Him by, too?

Shortly before He died, He ate supper with His disciples. He took bread, broke it, blessed it, and gave it to His disciples. He said, "This is like my body which will be broken for you. Eat all of it." Then He took a cup (filled with some kind of grape juice) and passed it to His disciples. "This is like my blood which will be shed for your sins. Drink all of it."

So everytime Christians celebrate the Lord's Supper (Communion), they remember and are thankful that Jesus died for them. They will do this until Jesus comes again.

*Bible Verse:* "For as often as you eat this bread and drink this cup you show people that you remember the Lord's death till he comes again" (1 Cor. 11:26).

*Prayer:* Dear Jesus, thank you for coming to earth to die for our sins. Thank you for giving us the Lord's Supper as a remembrance of you. Help us to deserve your love. Amen.

## Rainbow Means Promise

Do you know what a rainbow is? Do you know when it appeared in the sky for the first time and why?

A rainbow is an arch (part of a circle) of brilliant colors that appears in the sky after a shower of rain. It is seen in the sky opposite the sun. If the rain has been heavy, the bow may form a half circle so that its two ends look as if they touch the ground.

When the sun's rays pass through the drops of rain, their colors are bent (refracted) and separated into bands of colors in the sky.

After the great Flood God placed the rainbow in the sky as a reminder to Noah that He would never again destroy the earth with a flood.

God has kept that promise. He has kept other promises, too. He promised Moses He would help the Jews escape from Egypt, and He did. He promised to send Jesus to be our Savior. He said Jesus would be born in Bethlehem and that He would die for our sins. These things happened just as God said they would.

*Something to Think About:* Can you trust all people? Why not?

Can you think of other promises that God made and kept?

Jesus promised that He would come back to earth again. At that time He will take those who love Him to heaven to live with Him forever. Has this happened? Can you believe that it will? Why?

*Bible Verse:* "There has not failed one word of all God's promises" (1 Kings 8:56).

"And what God has promised he will do" (Rom. 4:21).

*Prayer:* Dear Lord God, we are glad that we can trust you to keep your promises. Help us to keep our promises too. Amen.


# I Believe! I Believe!

Jon lives in Titusville, Florida. When he first moved there his parents took him and his sister, Dawn, to Cape Kennedy to watch the launchings of spacecrafts. He stood with his mouth open staring at the spacecraft that had been thrust into the air by rocket engines. He watched it climb higher and higher until he could see it no longer. Suddenly he became very frightened.

"Oh, Daddy," he said. "The astronauts have disappeared. Will they ever come back?"

"They'll come back; don't you worry," Daddy told Jon.

Some time later Jon and his dad watched the astronauts on television as they splashed down in the Pacific

Ocean. Jon sat on the edge of his chair as he watched the rescue helicopter pick them up and take them to a big ship that waited some miles away. When Jon saw that they were safely on board, he jumped to his feet and ran to his room. He returned with his Bible.

"Daddy, find the place where it tells about Jesus coming back to earth again."

Daddy found the place and read what the Bible said about Jesus leaving the earth after He rose from the grave on the first Easter Sunday. Then he read the verses that say Jesus is coming back to earth someday to take the people who love Him to be with Him forever.

"Now I believe it," Jon said. "I really do. It's just like the astronauts, only better because Jesus won't need a spacecraft or a helicopter."

*Something to Think About:* Ask your daddy or mother to read Acts 1:1-11 and John 4:2 and 3.

Do you believe Jesus will return someday as He said He would?

Who will live in the mansions Jesus is preparing in heaven?

What must we do so we will be ready when He comes?

*Bible Verse:* "Men of Galilee, why do you stand here staring into the sky? The same Jesus who has gone to heaven will someday come back again just as he went away" (Acts 1:11).

*Prayer:* Dear heavenly Father, thank you for making a world so wonderful that men can travel to the moon and come back again. Thank you for sending your Son to this wonderful world to tell us about your great love. Help us to live so that we will be ready to meet Him when He comes back to earth again. Amen.

# It Makes a Difference

One day when the Vahlstrom family were eating dinner, they noticed that a fly clung to the ceiling at one end of the room. It did not move nor show any sign of life.

Jane, the oldest of the children, stared at it for some time. Then she said, "I think it's resting."

"Perhaps sleeping," Mother said.

"Dreaming, too," Mary added.

David, who was a couple of years younger, shook his head. "Nope," he said. "It's dead."

"Hanging from the ceiling like that?" Jane chided.

"Sure, he's got something sticky on his feet."

"Let's take a vote," Mother said. "Raise your hand if you think the fly is dead."

Only David raised his hand.

"I'll settle the question," Mr. Vahlstrom told his family. He went to the closet and came back with a yardstick. Standing on tiptoe, he reached to touch the fly. But the moment it saw the yardstick, it took off and landed on a nearby windowpane.

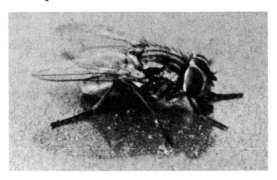

Mary turned to David. She wrinkled her nose. "See," she said, "it's not dead. It's alive."

Again David shook his head. "Nope! It's dead!"

*Something to Think About:* Why do you think David kept saying the fly was dead even though he had seen it fly? Did he really believe the fly was dead?

Of course not.

Yet, though Jesus showed himself to many people after He rose from the dead, today there are still people who say they don't believe He did.

How do we know Jesus rose from the grave?

Why should we be glad He did?

*Bible Verse:* "Since we know that God raised Jesus from the grave, we can trust him to raise us, too" (2 Cor. 4:14).

"If you tell with your mouth and believe in your heart that God raised him [Jesus] from the dead, you shall be saved [you will prove that you belong to Jesus]" (Rom. 10:9).

*Prayer:* Dear God in heaven, thank you for raising Jesus from the grave. Thank you that we don't need to be afraid to die. We know that we will be raised someday, too. Help us to show our friends that we really believe this is true. Amen.

## Who's Who in Heaven

"Hey, Keith," George Adams called. "My mom just told me something. Did you know your dad's name is in *Who's Who?*"

"*Who's Who?*" What's that?" Keith asked.

"I don't know exactly. I think it's some kind of a book that has the names of all the important people in our country."

Later Keith asked his dad about his name being in the *Who's Who* book. "Is that true?"

"Yes, it is true," Keith's father answered. "But, Keith, that doesn't mean nearly as much to me as knowing my name is in God's *Who's Who* book in heaven."

*Something to Think About:* When Jesus told His disciples that they would be able to do many things in His name, He told them this wasn't as important as having their names in God's book in heaven. The Bible calls heaven's *Who's Who* book the "book of life."

Do you know how you can get your names in God's book of life? (By becoming Christians.)

*Bible Verse:* "Rejoice [be glad] because your names are written in heaven" (Luke 10:20).

*Prayer:* Dear God, we thank you because you know each one who belongs to you. Help us to understand that having our names in your "book of life" is more important than anything that can happen to us. Amen.


## What's a Flashlight For?

One Sunday Dick Barber's pastor talked about the Bible. He told the people the Bible was made up of 66 books and that even though they were written by 40 different people, they all talked about the same God and His love.

The pastor said the Bible is the story of man. It tells how God took care of His people in olden times and how He takes care of them now. He said, "The Bible is many things. It is God's word; it is sometimes thought of as bread. And it is a light. We could call it a flashlight."

*Something to Think About:* Think of all the uses for a flashlight: Finding one's way in the dark; hunting for something that is lost; it can be used as a signal that warns others of danger; or as a light when electric lights go out; as a bicycle light.

How is the Bible like a flashlight?

*Bible Verse:* "Thy word is a lamp for my feet, a light for my path" (Ps. 119:105).

*Prayer:* Dear God, thank you for the Bible. Thank you because it teaches us about your love. Thank you that it warns us against sin. Help us to memorize it more than we do. Amen.

## A Mind Is to Use

Mr. and Mrs. Brown were worried about their daughter Becky's school work. She didn't seem to care whether she learned anything or not. Her teacher said she was bright and that she could do much better work than she was doing.

Finally Mr. Brown said he had had enough of her foolishness. "You bring home a good report card or we won't go to Disneyland," he told her.

Becky wanted to go to Disneyland. She studied hard for a while. But before long she grew careless again. Then

report time arrived. She had to think of something to do.

That evening when she handed her father the report-card envelope, he opened it and took out the card which he studied carefully. "Hmmmmm!" he said, a pleased sound in his voice. "Not bad."

Suddenly his face changed. He stared at the report card as if he were seeing it for the first time. "What's the meaning of this?" he asked. "You gave me Cheryl Smith's card."

Becky shifted from one foot to the other. "I asked her if I could borrow it. You said I had to bring a good report card home . . . so I did."

*Something to Think About:* What do you think of Becky's scheme? Honest? No. Clever? Yes. But does that excuse Becky?

Who is to blame for her poor report card?

*Bible Verse:* "If I have failed, I am the one who is to blame" (Job 19:4).

"He who is slothful [lazy] in his work is a brother of a waster" (Prov. 18:9).

*Prayer:* Dear Father in heaven, thank you for giving us minds with which to think and study. Help us to use them as well as we can. Forgive us when we don't do as good work as we are able to do. Amen.

## "Look Up!"

Jimmy and Brian pedaled their bikes lazily along the country road.

Suddenly Jimmy braked his bike. "Stop!" he shouted. Brian stopped. "Look!" Jimmy pointed to a field where fat watermelons lay soaking up the warm California sun.

The boys laid their bikes down on the shoulder of the road and headed for the watermelon patch.

Running ahead, Jimmy reached it first. He tapped his knuckles against one of the melons. He stooped to pick it up. Then he stopped. Quickly he looked to the right, then to the left. He looked in front of him. He looked behind him. Once again he stooped to pick up the watermelon.

"Wait!" Brian called.

"What for?" Jimmy asked.

"You forgot to look up!"

*Something to Think About:* What did Brian mean when he told Jimmy, "You forgot to look up"?

Why was it important that Jimmy remember to look up?

Is it ever right to do wrong because no other person sees you?

*Bible Verse:* "The eyes of the Lord are in every place. He sees both the good and the bad" (Prov. 15:3).

*Prayer:* Dear God, we love you. We know that you are everywhere and that you see everything we do. You hear everything we say. Please help us remember that you know all about us even if other people don't. Amen.

## A Different Birthday Party

Beth Taylor was five years old. Soon she would be six. "Will we have a birthday party?" Beth asked her mother.

"We always do."

"And may I invite anyone I want to?"

"If you like."

"How many may I ask?" Beth wanted to know.

"Eight would be a good number, don't you think? Your

birthday is on Saturday. We could begin the party at two o'clock in the afternoon. Okay?"

Beth thought that would be a good idea. And for days she planned whom she would invite to her party. She'd ask her best friend, Kathy Smith, and her cousin, Larry, and . . .

"Have you decided whom you are going to invite to your party?" Mother asked one day.

Beth nodded.

"Are you going to tell me?"

"It's a secret," Beth told her mother. "You said I could ask anyone I wanted to. You said eight people, and I asked eight people."

Mrs. Taylor smiled. She would let Beth keep her secret.

On Saturday, the day of Beth's birthday, Mother had everything ready. She had baked and decorated a cake. She had planned the games and bought prizes for the children. She was almost as excited as Beth. She could hardly wait to see whom her daughter had invited to her party.

At two o'clock the doorbell rang and one after the other of the guests arrived. Kathy Smith, Cousin Larry, and . . . Mother could hardly believe her eyes. Blind Mr. Thompson who lived down the street and Mrs. Cox, the woman who took care of him, came. Then the Marshall twins, Carla and Carmen, two black children from Beth's Sunday school class. Last of all, Grandmother and Grandfather Taylor arrived in a taxi from their home on the other side of town.

Together with Beth, Mother welcomed each one.

"Surprised?" Beth asked her mother.

Mother nodded. Then she gave Beth a big squeeze. "You are a dear child," she said.

*Something to Think About:* Why did Mrs. Taylor call Beth a dear child?

What made Beth's birthday party different from most children's parties?

Why do you think Beth invited these people to her party?

*Bible Verse:* "You should love your neighbor as yourself" (Matt. 22:39).

"This is my [Jesus'] commandment that you love others as I have loved you" (John 15:12).

"A friend loveth at all times" (Prov. 17:17).

*Prayer:* Dear Father God, thank you for this story. Thank you for Beth who loved her neighbor, her **black** friends, and others enough to invite them to her birthday party. Help us to show others that we love them as Jesus does too. Amen.

## My Dog's Better Than Your Dog

A television commercial tried to make listeners believe a dog was bigger, smarter, and healthier than other dogs because he ate a certain kind of dog food. The commercial usually began with some child saying, "My dog's better than your dog."

But it isn't only dog-food companies that boast like this. Listen:

> "My dad's stronger than your dad."
> "My mom's prettier than your mom."
> "I play ball better than you do."
> "I'm smarter than you are."
> "Our house is nicer than your house."

*Something to Think About:* What one word describes a person who thinks he is better than anyone else or one who boasts about his friends or the things he can do?

Could we say this person is proud?

The person who is the exact opposite from a proud person is called a *humble* person. He doesn't boast about what he can do and the things that he owns. He's thankful for them but never proud.

*Bible Verse:* "Whoever boasts he can do something he isn't able to do is like clouds and wind without rain" (Prov. 25:14).

"A man's pride will bring him low" (Prov. 29:23).

"For I say . . . to every man . . . not to think more highly of himself than he ought to think" (Rom. 12:3).

"Humble yourself [don't be proud]; then God will encourage and help you" (James 4:10).

*Prayer:* Dear Lord God, we know we have sinned against you many times by being boastful and proud. We have boasted about the things we can do and the things we own. Please forgive us. Help us to be kind, fair, and *humble*. Amen.


## Acorns and Pumpkins

Steve and Danny lay on the ground under an oak tree talking about birds, animals, trees, and plants that God created.

"I wonder why God made tiny acorns grow on big oak trees when He made big pumpkins grow on the ground," Steve said thoughtfully.

"That is funny, isn't it?" Danny answered.

Just then an acorn dropped off the oak tree above the boys. Plunk! It struck Steve's head and bounced onto the ground.

Danny began to laugh. "I guess God knew what He was doing, after all," he said. "What if that had been a pumpkin?"

*Something to Think About*: The Bible tells us that when God finished creating the world, He looked at it and saw that it was good.

Talk about some of the things God created that are wonderfully good (stars in the heavens; bees and their habits; how bats fly in the dark; how people can see and hear).

*Bible Verse*: "The heavens declare the glory of God, the earth shows the wonder of his creation" (Ps. 19:1).

"Let heaven and earth praise him, the seas, and everything that moves in them" (Ps. 69::34).

*Prayer:* Dear God, thank you for the wonderful world you created for us to live in. Help us to study all about it so we can understand it better. Amen.

## Grandparents!

The James family were discussing Grandmother's recent visit.

"I wish I hadn't been so busy," Mother said.

Mother had gone back to college when Cara, the youngest James' child, started kindergarten. Now she was almost through. Soon she would receive her teacher's degree.

"I wish those final exams hadn't come right in the middle of Gram's vacation," Mother added. "I'm sorry I had to do so much studying."

"I don't think you need to worry," Mr. James told his wife. "The kids did a good job of entertaining her."

"I know." Mother looked at Cara, then at the two older children, Enid and David. "You were great."

"It was fun," David said.

"Sometimes," Enid added.

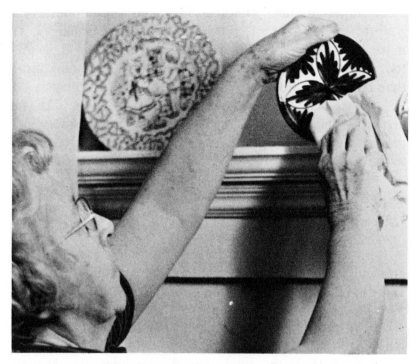

Mother raised her eyebrows.

"Well, you know how grandmothers are. '*I think you should do it this way....*'" Dana's voice sounded just like Grandmother's. "'*I always stack the dishes before I wash them. Sheets should be tucked in this way. Here, let me show you.*' And sometimes she didn't like the way we talked. She said, '*Not ain't, isn't, Dana.*'"

"So what?" David stopped her. He turned to his mother. "Don't pay any attention to her, Mom."

Mother laughed. "Didn't she ever bug you?"

"Not very often. You see, I decided she's lived a lot longer than we have. So she ought to know how to do things. Besides, she's a good storyteller. She told us what things were like when she was our age. Neat!"

*Something to Think About*: People who understand families believe that children need grandparents just as much as grandparents need children. Most often they relate very well to each other. Besides, grandparents usually have more time to read to children. They have time to listen, too. And when you really think about it, they know more than children do, too.

Do you have grandparents who live near you? If you do, show them how much you love them. If your grandparents live far away, remember they may be lonely. Write to them often.

When the apostle Paul wrote to Timothy, he spoke of the young man's faith in Jesus (2 Tim. 3:15) which, Paul said, he had learned in his childhood, from his grandmother, Lois, and his mother, Eunice.

*Bible Verse:* "Honor [respect and love] your father and mother [and your grandfather and grandmother]; then you will be rewarded with a long life" (Ex. 20:12).

*Prayer:* Dear Lord, thank you for mothers and fathers who love you. Thank you for grandfathers and grandmothers who love you too. Thank you for all grandfathers and grandmothers. If there are some who do not love you, we pray that someone will tell them about you. Be with our grandparents today. In Jesus' name, amen.

## Hear and Listen!

The Winter family vacationed at their ocean cottage each summer. Heather and her sister, Ruth, enjoyed going to the ocean. They especially liked the beach. They played in the sand for hours at a time. They built castles with high towers. They dug trenches around the castle and filled them with water. They pretended these trenches were moats which would keep enemies from entering their castles.

Sometimes they waded or swam in the ocean. Sometimes they hunted for shells and driftwood. At other times they raced to see who could run faster from one place to another—always staying in plain sight of their cottage where Father and Mother said it was safe to race.

One day Ruth didn't feel very well. Mother decided to keep her in the house for the day.

Heather played in the sand by herself for a while. Then she decided to run along the beach even if Ruth wasn't there to race with her. Without realizing it, she ran farther than she should have.

Mother saw what she had done. She cupped her hands around her mouth and called, "Heather! Heather!" Heather kept on running. "Heather! Heather! Come back!" By now Heather was out of range of her mother's voice.

When Heather returned Mother said, "Why didn't you come when I called? Didn't you hear me?"

Heather didn't answer at once. When she did she spoke softly, for she was ashamed. "I heard you, Mother, but I wasn't listening."

*Something to Think About:* Have you ever done what Heather did? Is it possible to hear and not listen? Explain your answer.

Most of us know that it isn't only Mother we so often hear but fail to listen to. In each of us is a still, small voice called our *conscience* that tells us what is right and what is wrong. Even if Heather hadn't heard her mother's voice, we can believe she would have heard her conscience tell her she was running too far from the house. But to obey her conscience she would have had to listen to it too.

We must remember that everyone doesn't have the same kind of conscience. Some children don't know what is wrong and what is right because they have never been taught the difference. Others never pay any attention to their consciences. In time they won't be able to hear it at all. You can trust your conscience if you let God control it.

*Bible Verse:* "He who belongs to God hears [and listens] to God's words" (John 8:47).

"Whosoever hearkens [gives careful attention] to God need not fear evil" (Prov. 1:33).

"He who hearkens to good advice is wise" (Prov. 12:15).

"A wise son [or daughter] heareth [listens and follows] his father's instructions" (Prov. 13:1).

*Prayer:* Dear Father in heaven, give us each the kind of conscience that is quick to understand what is right and what is wrong. Help us to listen to what our conscience says. Forgive us for the times we have acted like Heather. Amen.

## Sometimes We Need To Be Afraid

Mrs. Barry took her three small children—Mark, 6, Susie, 4, and Merilee, 2—to the park to play. Mark and Susie headed for the slide. Merilee toddled off toward the sandbox. Mother sat down on a bench to watch her children.

Before long Mark and Susie tired of the slide. "Come push me, Mother," Susie called as they ran toward the swings.

"I'll be right with you," Mother answered.

She pushed Susie up, up, higher, higher. Suddenly Mark shouted, "Merilee! Watch out!"

Mother stopped the swing and turned to see what Merilee was doing. She gasped. Merilee had climbed half way to the top of the slide. As she turned to look at Mark her foot slipped, and she tumbled to the ground.

Mother rushed to pick her up. When she saw that Merilee

wasn't hurt, she scolded her for trying to climb the slide.

Later at home, Mark and Susie heard their parents talking about the fall. Mother said, "Bless her heart, she doesn't know enough to be afraid."

*Something to Think About:* It's true small children sometimes don't know enough to be afraid. Can you name some of the things they should be afraid of? (Touching a stove; going too far from shore when they don't know how to swim; crossing a busy street; climbing too high; playing with matches.)

What are some of the things older children should be afraid of? (Drugs, cigarettes, liquor, swearing, stealing, the wrong kinds of friends, hate, jealousy.)

*Bible Verse:* "Fear him who is able to destroy your soul and body . . ." (Matt. 10:28).

"Seeing you know these things beware [be afraid] of those who teach things that are not true to the teachings of Jesus" (Col. 2:8).

"A wise man feareth [is afraid] and stays away from sin" (Prov. 14:16).

*Prayer:* Dear Lord, help us to learn which things we should be afraid of. Help us to run away from the things that would hurt our bodies, our minds, or our souls. Amen.

## Big Words for Sin

Andre is a boy who likes to tease. One day he went up to his algebra teacher. "Can a student be punished for something he didn't do?" he asked.

His teacher, a tall, lanky fellow, thought for a minute; then he said, "I guess I'll have to say *no* to that question."

Andre's dark eyes sparkled mischievously. "Good," he

exclaimed; "then I won't be punished for not doing my algebra assignment."

*Something to Think About:* What do you think about this story?

Would it be right for teachers to excuse students who don't do their homework? Why?

Some people think we sin only when we do something wrong. But the Bible teaches that we also sin when we fail to do something good that we know we ought to do.

Things that we do that are wrong are called sins of *commission* (an act of doing). Failing to do something good that we know we ought to do is called a sin of *omission* (not doing).

*Bible Verse:* "To him who knows to do good and then doesn't do it, to him it is sin" (James 4:17).

*Prayer:* Dear Jesus, we often ask you to forgive the bad things we do. Now we have learned we should ask you to forgive us for not doing things we know we ought to do. One of our friends may be sick; we don't visit him. A kid tells a dirty story, and we don't tell him to stop. We don't always let our school friends know we love you. Someone may hurt us and say he is sorry. We stay mad at him. Please forgive us for these sins. Help us to remember the lesson we learned today. Amen.

## Out of Focus

Father set up the slide projector. He put the vacation slides in the machine. Then he connected the machine and flipped the switch.

The first pictures were so fuzzy that Sally and Jimmy couldn't tell what they were. Father made some adjustments—but still the pictures didn't clear up.

"They are out of focus," Father said. "I guess I must have moved the camera, or else I didn't set it right."

A few days later Jimmy came home from school pouting. He had missed several words in his spelling test. "What's the matter with you?" Mother asked.

Jimmy didn't answer. Instead he went to his room and slammed the door. Mother followed him.

"Well," she said. "I guess pictures aren't the only things that can get out of focus." Jimmy looked at her, wondering what she meant. Then he saw she had a teasing smile on her lips. Now he understood. He began to laugh. Mother laughed too. And ever since that day whenever someone in the family pouts or doesn't behave as he should, a member of the family shouts, "Out of focus!"

*Something to Think About:* When we pout or do things we shouldn't, our lives are fuzzy (out of focus).

Are you ever out of focus?

Which of the following children would you say are "out of focus"?

1. Dad asks his son John to mow the lawn. John mows the lawn, but he lets everyone know he didn't want to. When his friends come to play ball, he grumbles because he can't go with them.

2. Bob's grandfather gives him an extra quarter to put in the Sunday school offering plate. A friend says, "Why don't you spend the money for something you want? Your grandfather will never know."

"But I will know. And God will know," Bob answers. "And the money belongs to God. Grandpa said so."

3. Mother asks Jerry to run to the store to get her some baking powder. "I need it right now," she says.

Jerry, who is working on an airplane model, doesn't like to be disturbed. "Okay, okay," he mutters, as he gets to his feet and starts down the street as if he has all the time in the world.

4. Judy is a guest at Anne's home. Anne's mother serves a new casserole dish for dinner. It has spinach and broccoli in it. Judy doesn't care very much about these vegetables, but she eats some of the casserole anyway. *Maybe,* she thinks, *I'll learn to like spinach someday.*

*Bible Verse:* "Even a child is known by his doings, whether his life is good and whether it is right" (Prov. 20:11).

*Prayer:* Dear Jesus, we love you because you are always kind and good. Your life is never out of focus. Help us this day to live so that people can tell that our lives are "in focus" because we belong to you. Amen.

## Pollyanna

Pollyanna is the name of the main character in a book written by Eleanor H. Porter many years ago. In the story Pollyanna plays a "never sad" game with herself. Though many bad things happen to her, she always pretends there is nothing wrong.

Paul, one of Jesus' disciples, had bad things happen to him, too. He was beaten and stoned. He was put in prison. Some people believe his eyesight was very poor. Jesus suffered when He lived on earth, too. He also was stoned and beaten. Finally He was put to death on a cross.

But Jesus and Paul didn't pretend these things hadn't happened. Instead they thanked and praised God for them. They told us to praise and thank God too. Not because of the bad things that happen to us, but because we have a God who will make something good out of the bad, a God who will comfort, love, and help us every day.

*Bible Verse:* "Rejoice in the Lord always, and again I say, Rejoice" (Phil. 4:4).

"And we know that all things work together for good to them that love God" (Rom. 8:28).

*Prayer:* Dear Jesus, we thank you that you promised that you will help us in our problems. We understand that just as you had trouble and trials we will have them too. Help us to show people by a happy attitude that we love and trust you to work everything out for good. Amen.

## What Kind of a Job Is That?

Clark Percy's father was a church custodian. He kept the church sparkling clean and everything neatly in place.

He went to church early to unlock the doors before each service. He always checked each one to be sure it was locked before he went home.

Often when he was tired he went into the sanctuary (worship area) and prayed. He thanked God for all His goodness. Then he prayed for the choir members, the Sunday school teachers, missionaries the church supported, the pastor and members of the church.

One day Clark and some of his friends were talking about what they'd like to be when they grew up. One of the boys wanted to be a banker and make a lot of money. Another wanted to be a mechanical engineer; another, an astronaut. When it was Clark's turn, he said, "I want to be a church custodian like my dad."

The boys looked at him, surprised. "Are you nuts?" the want-to-be-a-banker boy said. "What kind of a job is that?"

*Something to Think About:* Who is your hero? What person do you look up to and wish to grow up to be like? Why?

Does a person have to do a certain kind of work to be respected and liked? Is a person who works with his hands less important than one who works with his mind?

Did you know that there is a verse in the Bible that talks about church custodians?

*Bible Verse:* "I'd rather be a doorkeeper in the house of the Lord than to live in tents of wickedness [places of sin]" (Ps. 84:10).

"It is better to wish to have a good name than it is to wish to become rich" (Prov. 22:1).

*Prayer:* Dear Jesus, we've never really thought much about church custodians and all the work they do. Today we want to thank you for our church custodian. Help us to show him (or her) that we appreciate what he does for us. Show us what you want us to do when we grow up.

Help us to love people no matter what kind of work they do. Amen.


## "We Are Rich!"

---

Jennie Sellers would never forget the day Mr. Glen MacDaniels telephoned her father's hardware store from San Francisco. He and his wife were going to be passing through the town where the Sellers lived and would stop to say hello.

Mr. Sellers told his clerks to take care of things at the store; then he hurried home to tell the family the news.

What commotion! Jennie's mother had just finished painting the crib for the baby who would be born in a few weeks. She had paint on her hands, on her clothes, and in her hair. Her husband didn't seem to mind. He hugged her and said, "Go clean up. I'll give the house a quick checkup."

"But, Tom," Mrs. Sellers began, "those people! I'm scared."

Jennie knew what she meant. The MacDaniels were very rich. Father had often talked about them. They had been classmates with him in college, and now Mr. Mac-Daniels had a job that took them all over the world.

Jennie and her parents lived in a very ordinary home. They didn't have fancy furniture or clothes. That was because most of the money Mr. Sellers made was used to pay for the hardware store he was buying.

Before they were really ready, the MacDaniels arrived —dressed like the mannequins in San Francisco's *I. Magnin* store windows. Because it was warm, Jennie's father asked them to visit on the patio. He had forgotten all about the paint cans and the newly painted crib.

"Getting ready for the new baby, I see," Glen Mac-Daniels said. "You are lucky people. I wish . . ." He stopped. "We've never had any children."

"It just wouldn't work out," his wife added, "traveling all the time as we do."

When Mr. Sellers asked his friends to stay for supper, Mr. MacDaniels seemed to want to. But his wife said, "We'd better be on our way."

After they had driven away, Jennie's father took her mother into his arms. "Honey," he said, "I promise. Someday *we'll* be rich . . ."

Quickly Mother pulled away from him. She looked around the room—at the picture of Jesus hanging above the fireplace, at the Bible on the coffee table, and then at Jennie.

"Listen, mister, we are rich!" she said. "It doesn't matter if we never have extra money."

*Something to Think About:* What did Jennie's mother mean when she said they were rich?

Can people be rich even if they don't have a great deal of money? How?

*Bible Verse:* "A man is a fool if he gathers wealth for himself and is not rich toward God" (Luke 12:21).

"Has not God chosen the poor in this world who are rich in faith?" (James 2:5).

"Tell the rich . . . not to trust in uncertain riches but in the living God" (1 Tim. 6:17).

"Though he [Christ] was rich, yet for your sakes he became poor that you through his poverty might become rich" (2 Cor. 8:9).

*Prayer:* Dear Lord, thank you for leaving your home in heaven to become poor so that we could become rich in the things that really count. We know that you had rich friends as well as poor friends, yet you told all of them that to be truly rich they needed to belong to you. Help us never to forget that our faith is the only wealth that counts. Amen.

## A Very Special Child

Gwen and Darcy were playing ball with the neighbor children, Billy and Lana. Holly, who was Gwen and Darcy's younger sister, was not very bright. But she liked to play too.

Once when Billy threw a ball to Darcy she missed it. Quickly Holly ran to pick it up.

"Holly play," she said.

Billy clenched his fists. "Here we go again," he said.

"She only wants to play," Gwen told him.

"Sure, but does she know how? Of course not. That's because she's crazy."

"You wouldn't know how to play very well if you were born that way," Darcy answered.

"Just a crazy kid!" Billy muttered.

Gwen walked over to Holly and put her arm around her. She turned to Billy. "I think you should go," she said. "We'll play some other day."

*Something to Think About:* Holly was what is called a mongoloid child. She is retarded (doesn't learn as quickly as other children) because of an accidental arrangement of chromosomes in her body.

Our bodies are made up of billions of tiny cells. Chromosomes are very small parts of these cells. They determine the color of our hair and eyes, how tall we will be, whether we will be a girl or a boy, whether we will learn quickly or slowly. Each cell has forty-six chromosomes. Holly was born with forty-seven. Children like Holly are usually loving, kind, and gentle. They should be given special love because they are special children.

Did you notice how Gwen and Darcy showed they loved Holly?

There are other children who have different learning problems than Holly. They need special love and care too.

*Bible Verse:* "Comfort [love] the feeble minded [the retarded], take care of the weak, and be patient with everyone" (1 Thess. 5:14).

*Prayer:* We don't know just how to pray today. Often we have seen boys and girls who weren't very bright and instead of loving them, we stared at them or just left them by themselves. We've heard children who made fun of retarded children just as Billy made fun of Holly. But we didn't stop them. Please forgive us. Help us to love them as you do, Amen.

## Shhhhh!

A very kind old man loved his church, the house of God, where he worshipped every Sunday. He felt badly when children or young people were noisy, played tag or raced through the church when meetings were over.

One day he mustered up enough courage to say, "Shhhhh! This is God's house. You should respect and honor it."

A teenager laughed at the old man. "It's just an old building," he said. "What's so special about some bricks and wood?"

*Something to Think About:* What do you think? Do you believe your church is just a building like any other

building or do you love and respect it as a special place to worship God?

What do you do when you come to church? Do you sit quietly? Do you pray and ask God to bless the service or do you laugh and chat with your friends? Do you race through the church when meetings are dismissed?

*Bible Verse:* "The Lord is in his holy temple [church]; let all the earth keep silent before him" (Hab. 2:20).

"Respect God's house [the place where you worship God]" (Lev. 19:30).

*Prayer:* Dear Lord, we are often careless about the way we behave when we are in your house. Please forgive us. Help us to worship you quietly and reverently, remembering that you are a holy God. Amen.

## "I Never Cry!"

Paula lived in a small town only a block from the family's dentist. When she was very small Mother took her to the dentist whenever she needed to have her teeth checked.

The day came, though, when Paula thought she was old enough to go to the dentist alone. Since it was safe for her to do so, Mother said she could.

One day, Paula had one of her baby teeth pulled. When she came home, Mother asked, "Did you cry?"

"Mother!" Paula answered disgustedly. "You know I never cry."

*Something to Think About:* Can you guess what Mother said then?

She took Paula into her arms. She said, "Honey, don't ever be ashamed to cry."

We know we aren't meant to be "cry babies," crying for every little thing that happens to us. But we have a right to cry when we hurt badly, when we are sorry for some wrong we have done, or when we are sad.

The Bible tells us it is natural for us to cry when someone we love dies even though we know that person has gone to be with God. We will miss this person, and we should cry because for some strange reason tears help heal the hurt.

Jesus wept when His friend Lazarus died. He wept, too, when he looked at the city of Jerusalem and realized that so many who lived in the city didn't understand or believe the things He had told them.

After it had been decided that Jesus should be put to

death, Peter cried because he realized he had sinned when he denied he knew the Lord.

In Egypt Joseph cried because he was so glad to see his brothers.

We should remember, though, that tears belong to this life only. Why?

*Bible Verse:* "Jesus wept" (John 11:35).

" . . . [in heaven] God shall wipe all tears from their eyes" (Rev. 7:17).

*Prayer:* Thank you for helping us understand when it is right to cry. Thank you for giving us tears to help heal our hurt. Amen.

## Forgive and Be Forgiven

When Leonardo da Vinci, the famous artist, was painting the *Last Supper*, he had a terrible quarrel with an old friend.

He was so miserable and unhappy that he found he just couldn't paint the face of Jesus. Every time he tried, he had to stop. Then one day he realized what he should do.

Though he hadn't started the quarrel, he went to his friend and asked him to forgive him. When things were made right between the two, Leonardo da Vinci found he could paint again.

*Something to Think About:* What does it mean to forgive?

What does it mean to be forgiven?

You may wonder why Leonardo felt better after he had asked his friend to forgive him when he wasn't the one to blame for the quarrel. The Bible tells us this is the right thing to do. Only then can we be happy and at peace with ourselves and God.

*Bible Verse:* "If you forgive men when they have wronged you, your heavenly father will forgive you" (Matt. 6:14).

"And when you stand praying, forgive the person who has wronged you so God can forgive you" (Luke 11:4).

"Be kind to one another, tenderhearted, forgiving one another. Even as Christ forgave you, so you must also do" (Eph. 4:32).

*Prayer:* Dear Lord God, sometimes it is easier to forgive someone than it is to ask for forgiveness. It's especially hard to ask forgiveness of someone who has hurt us badly. But we must if we want you to forgive us. Help us not to hold grudges. Help us to be forgiving people. Amen.

## Homing Instinct

*The Incredible Journey,* a book by Sheila Burnford, is a story about two dogs, a Labrador and a terrier, and a Siamese cat. When their owners went to Europe for a year, they left the animals with a friend who lived nearly three hundred miles away.

Just before the owners came back, the man who took care of them went on a hunting trip. He asked his housekeeper to feed them while he was gone. But before he left he let the animals out for their morning run. Then he drove off in his car for his hunting trip. The animals didn't stay at the house, though. Instead they began a long, hard trip back to their real home.

The cat and the dogs stayed away from the main roads. They cut straight across rough wilderness country. On the

143

trip they had all kinds of trouble. They fought wild animals. They got hurt. They were often hungry and tired, but they kept going.

When all of the people were sure that the animals were lost forever, they came trudging home.

*Something to Think About:* How did they know where to go?

We don't know, except that we believe God gives birds and animals a special kind of sense that helps them find their way from place to place. We call that sense *instinct*.

Like the animals who had a part-time home and a real home, we have two homes too. We have a home here on earth and we have one in heaven. Jesus said, "In my father's house are many mansions. I go to prepare a place for you. . . ."

If we love Jesus, the homing instinct He gives us will help us stay on the path that leads to this heavenly home.

*Bible Verse:* "Father, I [Jesus] want these who believe in me to be where I am" (John 17:24).

"I [Paul] would rather leave this world to be with the Lord" (2 Cor. 5:8).

"For to live here is to live for Christ, but to die is gain. I am torn between wanting to stay on earth and wanting to go to heaven, which is far better" (Phil. 1:21-23).

*Prayer:* Dear Jesus, thank you for preparing a place for us in heaven. Help us to be like the animals in the story. They didn't let anything stop them from finding their real home. Help us not to let anything come into our lives that would stop us from reaching our heavenly home. Amen.

## The Lost Chance

What? Gloria Simons squeezed her eyes closed and bit her lip hard. Heather West! The new pianist for the Junior High Choir! *Why her?* Gloria thought, remembering how badly she had wanted the job.

That night she told her mother about her disappointment. "I've taken piano lessons just as long as she has," Gloria said.

"Did they have tryouts?" her mother asked.

"Of course."

"Did you hear Heather play?"

"No. We tried out alone.

"Gloria, do me a favor?" her mother asked. "Don't tell anyone how you feel. Just listen to Heather play. Okay?"

"Okay," Gloria answered glumly.

When the choir met for practice, Gloria listened carefully as Heather played. Then shame washed over her. She had to admit that Heather played much better than she did. *I wonder why?*

Later Gloria met Heather. She said, "Congratulations, Heather. How did you learn to play like that?"

Heather laughed. "Practice and more practice! Mother kept after me. But I'm glad she did. And my dad! He kept saying, 'You have to practice what you want to reach.'"

Gloria's mother had kept after her too. But she hadn't listened. She thought of the many lessons she had missed because she didn't know her lesson.

"You have to practice what you want to reach. And I never really tried," Gloria told herself.

*Something to Think About:* If you want to be a good reader, what must you do?

If you want to be a good singer, what must you do?

If you want to be a good Christian, what must you do?

*Bible Verse:* "Whatever your hand finds to do, do it with all your might" (Eccles. 9:10).

"He that is slothful [lazy] in his work is brother to the person who is a waster" (Prov. 18:9).

*Prayer:* Dear Lord, we are ashamed too. There are so many things that we could do better, but we don't practice doing them. Forgive us. Point out the talents you want us to use for you. Help us to develop them through practice so we can do them well. Amen.

## "I'll Kill You!"

---

In the kitchen Timothy Edward picked up the popcorn his mother had made for him before she left to visit a neighbor who was ill. He headed for the family room. There he turned on the television and settled himself on the floor to watch his favorite program. It was about different kinds of untamed animals and birds.

When the program ended, a program about bad men followed it. Tim didn't turn off the set, though his mother had said he should. "I'll watch it for a few minutes," he told himself; "then I'll turn it off." But he became so interested in the excitement of the program that he forgot. And right in the middle of a wild desert chase where one man shouted, "Stop, or I'll kill you!" Tim heard his mother's voice.

"Timothy . . ."

Tim jumped to his feet and pressed the button that turned off the television. Blushing, he turned to his mother. "I . . ." He couldn't say anything. What was there to say? He had disobeyed her.

Mrs. Brown took off her coat and sat down on the davenport. "Come here," she said. Tim crossed the room and joined his mother. She cleared her throat. "Tim, do you remember the time when you were little when you accidentally closed the garage door on your pet kitten?"

Tim nodded. How could he forget? He'd felt so badly that he had had to force himself to go to school that day. Later just thinking about the kitten made him sick to his stomach. He vomited and had to be sent home from school. Now he felt sick all over again just thinking about it.

"Tim," his mother said quietly, "if you felt so badly about a little kitten's death, how can you stand to watch people being killed?"

"But it's only pretend."

"And you like to pretend that real people get shot and killed?"

His mother understood him too well. He had begun to like these programs. *Could that be wrong?* Tim wondered. What could he say?

*Something to Think About:* We call arson (fire that is set on purpose) and shooting and killing *violence*. Today more and more people are being killed, really killed, for no reason at all on the streets and in homes. Why do you suppose this is happening?

Many people believe violence is learned when boys and girls watch violent television programs. Do you watch violence on your TV? Have such programs affected you as they did Tim? Have you begun to like them too?

*Bible Verse:* "If you are guilty of wrongdoing, stop; don't let wickedness [which would include violence] be a part of your home" (Job 11:14).

*Prayer:* Dear Lord, you know when we watch violent television programs. Please forgive us. Help us to choose programs that are good and worthwhile. Be with television producers. Help them plan programs that will help us and not hurt us. Keep us from ever being violent. Amen.

## Perfect Pitch

The Bible says that God gives each one of us a special talent to use for Him. He gave Lona Jordan perfect pitch. This means that she can sing any musical note she wants to perfectly without any help from anyone. In school if her teacher wants the class to sing a song that starts on middle C, Lona sings "do-o-o" and the teacher can be sure she has pitched the song right on middle C.

Few people have perfect pitch. Some may be able to paint or draw. Others may be very mechanical. A doctor who is good with his hands may be able to perform operations well.

The Bible talks about other types of gifts that can be used in our work for Him, too. Some people are given the gift of preaching. Others receive the gift of teaching. Some are given the gift of helping (which means they can use any one of the talents they own). Others are given the gift of being able to speak in other languages.

*Bible Verse:* "And God gives some people the gift of evangelism, preaching, or teaching. Some receive the gift of healing, others the gift of helping or the ability to speak in other languages" (paraphrase of Eph. 4 and 2 Cor. 12).

*Prayer:* Dear Lord, thank you for the many different gifts and talents you give to people. Thank you for the gift of evangelism you have given Billy Graham. Thank you for the gift of preaching you gave our pastor. Thank you for those who have perfect pitch, or can paint and draw, or fix things so they can help other people. Please help us discover what special gifts you have given us. Then help us to use them for you. Amen.

## It's on the Way

Leslie Greggor thought he had brought enough money with him to cover all his expenses at Bible camp. One morning the craft teacher told him he would need another dollar to pay for material for a leather project. Leslie wanted to work on the project, but he didn't have another dollar.

"I know what I'll do," he told his bunk partner, Bob James. "I'll write and ask my father for a dollar." After he had written the letter he told the craft teacher he would pay him in a couple of days. "I wrote a letter asking my father for the money," he said.

"How do you know he will send it?" the man asked.

"He always says he will listen to a 'reasonable request.' And I'm sure he will think this one is reasonable."

Leslie was right. When his father received his letter, he put a dollar in an envelope and mailed it to his son.

The day after Leslie had sent his first letter he sat down and wrote his father another one. "Asking for more money?" Bob asked him.

"Nope, I'm just thanking Dad for the money he sent."

"The money he sent? It hasn't even come yet."

"I know. There hasn't been enough time. But it will come. I know my dad. I'm sure he's already sent it."

*Something to Think About:* God is like this father. We are His children just as Leslie was Mr. Greggor's son. God

will answer our "reasonable requests" too. What is a reasonable request?

Usually we thank someone for a gift *after* it has been received. Leslie thanked his father for the money *before* it arrived. Does God expect us to do the same thing?

*Bible Verse:* "In everything by prayer and supplication [asking] with thanksgiving let your requests be made known unto God" (Phil. 4:6).

*Prayer:* Thank you, God, for listening to our prayers. Thank you for answering "reasonable requests." Help us to be thankful when we pray. Teach us how to pray so that you will be pleased with us as your children. Amen.

## Mischief

"Have you seen Mischief?" Denise asked her mother. "She was in my room awhile ago, but I can't find her now."

"I put her outdoors some time ago," Mother answered. "I'm sure she'll soon want to come in."

"I think I'll try to find her," Denise answered.

Outside Denise called, "Come kitty; come kitty. Come, Mischief." She hurried across the lawn that sloped toward the creek back of the house. "Come kitty; come kitty." But no kitty came.

At dinner that night Denise kept her ear tuned for a "meow" that would tell her Mischief was back and wanted to come into the house. When the sun set Denise began to get worried. Her cat had never stayed out so late. "Daddy, do something. Find Mischief," she begged.

"Don't worry, honey," Daddy answered. "She'll be back anytime now."

"She'll come home when she gets hungry." Mother added.

"I'm going to ask God to find Mischief and send her home," Denise told her parents. And before Denise slept she prayed that Mischief would be back when she awakened the next morning.

Morning came, but still no Mischief. Denise called and called, but her cat didn't answer. Nor was she home when Denise came from school.

"Why didn't God answer my prayer?" Denise asked.

"He will," Mother answered. "Just remember He doesn't always answer *yes*. Sometimes He says *no* and sometimes He says *wait*."

"But He said 'if we believe.' I'm going to believe He will say *yes*."

Again that night Denise prayed. "Dear God, you know where Mischief is. Help her to find her way home. I know you can. In Jesus' name, amen." She crawled into bed and went to sleep believing God would answer her prayer.

"Meow! Meow!" Denise jumped out of bed. She threw on her robe and ran to the back door. There stood Mischief! She scooped her up in her arms. Turning she almost bumped into her mother who had come to see what happened.

"God heard me!" Denise shouted. "He answered my prayer."

"You're sure?" Mother asked.

"Yup! But first He said *wait*."

*Something to Think About:* Are all of your prayers answered?

Remember, prayers may be answered in three ways: *yes, no,* and *wait*. Most often we expect a *yes* answer. But we don't always get it. The Bible says there are several reasons why God sometimes answers *no*: When we ask for things we shouldn't ask for; when we have an unforgiving heart; when we have sin in our lives; or when God has something better He wants to give us.

*Bible Verse*: "Therefore I say to you, Whatsoever thing you desire when you pray, believe that you will receive them and you will have them" (Mark 11:24).

"If you abide in me and my words abide in you, you shall ask what you will and it shall be done for you" (John 15:7).

*Prayer:* Dear Lord Jesus, we know that everything we ask for may not be for our good. Help us to be sure we don't hold a grudge against anyone or have sin in our lives before we ask you for something. You know best what we ought to have. Help us to believe and trust you to give us what is best. Amen.

## All Better

Mae and her mother were visiting at a home that had a swimming pool. There were several young people in the pool. Mae watched them dive into the water. She watched them race across the pool.

All of a sudden she saw something strange. On a towel beside the pool lay a hand, all by itself.

"What's that, Mother?" she asked.

"That's Jerry Anderson's artificial hand," Mother answered. "It's called a *prosthesis*. You see, Jerry lost his own hand in an accident. A doctor made Jerry's artificial hand to look just like his real one. He never uses it when he swims. But he'll put it on when he comes out of the water."

Later when Jerry was dressed, Mae went over to him.

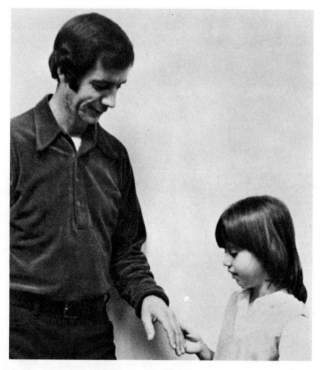

She touched the artificial hand lovingly. "It's all better now," she told Jerry.

*Something to Think About*: Who made the prosthesis for Jerry?

Have you ever thanked God for doctors who help make things "all better"?

Can you name other people for whom you should thank God?

*Bible Verse:* "In everything give thanks, for this is what God wants you to do" (1 Thess. 5:18).

*Prayer:* Dear God, our heavenly Father, thank you for doctors who have learned how to take good care of our bodies. Thank you for policemen who protect us. Thank you for people who write books for us to read. Thank you for farmers who grow our food. Thank you for everything. Amen.

# Want To Be Your Own Boss?

One morning when Tom's mother and dad took off on a business trip to Phoenix, Arizona, they left Tom's little sister, Grace, with Grandma. Tom, whom his parents trusted, stayed home to watch the house and to take care of his paper route.

Tom was glad they had left him at home—three whole days with no one to tell him what to do. He could go to bed when he wanted to; he could sleep as long as he liked. He could eat his favorite foods. No spinach! He could be his own boss!

After his parents left, Tom watched television for a while. He played ball with his friends. Then he called Jack, one of his friends, and asked him to go roller skating after lunch.

"This is wonderful," he told himself. And someday when he grew up it would always be like this. He'd be his own boss all the time.

Brrrring! The telephone broke into his thinking. It was his dad calling.

"Tom? Listen. I forgot some important papers at the office. Will you take your bike and go to the office and get them? Ask my secretary for the Adkins' file. Remember that? The *Adkins' file*. Have her put the papers in a box and wrap them well."

Tom wrote the name on a pad of paper by the phone.

"Then go to the bus depot. If you hurry you can make it before the bus leaves for Phoenix. Tell the agent in charge of deliveries that I'll pick up the papers at the bus depot there. Understand?"

"Will do," Gary told his father.

"Thank you, Son. I knew I could depend on you. 'Bye now."

Gary put the receiver back on the telephone. Then it hit him. The roller skating! He'd forgotten all about it. Oh, well. . . . He began to laugh.

Free? Was he? He picked up the phone and began to dial Jack's number. Free or not, he felt good inside. This is the way life is, he supposed. No one is ever free to do exactly as he pleases . . . and, who would want to be?

*Something to Think About:* Would you like to be your own boss?

Would you like to do exactly as you pleased? Is this ever possible?

Can children attend school, fathers work in offices, mothers in their homes without ever thinking about what other people want and need?

*Bible Verse:* "My son, listen to the instructions of your father, and don't fail to do what your mother tells you to do" (Prov. 1:8).

"Children, obey your parents in all things, for this is pleasing to God" (Col. 3:20).

"Don't talk back to those who are older than you, but treat them with respect" (1 Tim. 5:1).

"Tell others to obey government and officials [teachers, policemen, pastors, and others] who have authority over you" (Titus 3:1).

*Prayer:* Dear Lord, you know we often feel as Gary did. We want to be free to do exactly as we please. But we know this isn't possible. Each of us has responsibilities he must take care of. Help us to obey those who are supposed to lead and guide us. Most of all, help us to obey you. Amen.

## Kitty Did It

---

"Della!" Mother called from the kitchen where she was preparing dinner. "Stop tearing around."

"I'm only playing with Beige," Della answered from the

living room. Beige was Della's Siamese cat. She was given that name because of her yellow-brown color.

As she played, Della dangled a yo-yo in front of the cat. When Beige jumped and tried to reach the yo-yo, Della lifted it high above her head. Beige enjoyed playing with Della. She never seemed to tire of the fun. Once Della dropped the yo-yo. Beige ran, picked it up, and brought it back to her just as a dog would do.

Up and down, up and down, the yo-yo spun through the air. Suddenly Beige jumped higher than she had before. Della swung around, and the yo-yo flew out of her hand across the room. It landed behind the living room couch. Beige made a dash to find it. She jumped on a table beside the couch. Crash! The cat's tail hit the table lamp and knocked it off the table.

Mother came running. She gasped when she saw what had happened.

"Della, I told you. . . ."

"I didn't do it, honest, Mom. Kitty did it."

*Something to Think About:* Who really was to blame for the accident? Why?

It's easy to blame others for something we do that is wrong. Adam blamed Eve when he ate the fruit he was told not to eat. Aaron blamed the people of Israel because they worshipped a golden calf he had helped them make. Rather than take the blame for Jesus' death, Pilot planned a scheme so the people would demand that Jesus be put to death.

If you are ever tempted to blame someone else for something you do, remember that God knows who is to blame. But if we confess our sins and ask for forgiveness, the Bible tells us that God "will forgive them and remember them no more" (Heb. 10:17).

*Bible Verse:* "So everyone must give an account for himself before God" (Rom. 14:12).

"We will have to account for every idle [careless] word

we speak when we stand before God who is our judge" (Matt. 12:36).

*Prayer:* Dear Jesus, help us to remember the truth of these Bible verses. We thank you that we can come to you and ask for forgiveness. We thank you for forgiving the sins we confess and for forgetting them too. Amen.

## Tell It Like It Is

---

Quite by chance, Bruce Cummings happened to be the only one on the street corner when a bad accident happened. Because this was true, he was subpoenaed (called) to appear in court as a witness.

He was quite frightened when he stepped into the witness stand. The lawyer for the man Bruce thought was to blame for the accident stood ready to question him.

"Did anyone tell you what to say in court?" the lawyer asked.

"Yes, sir," Bruce answered.

"Aha, just as I thought," the lawyer said, a gleam in his eyes. "And who told you what to say?"

"My father did."

"He did? Now tell the court exactly what your father told you to say."

Bruce cleared his throat. He wanted to be sure he told the court exactly what his father had said he should.

"My father said the lawyers would try to mix me up. He said if I always told the truth I wouldn't have anything to worry about."

*Something to Think About*: What do you think of the answer Bruce gave the lawyer?

*Bible Verse*: "You should not bear [tell] false [untrue] witness" (Ex. 20:16).

"And the king said, 'How many times must I warn you to say nothing but the truth to me in the Lord?' " (2 Chron. 18:15).

"I speak the truth in Christ, and lie not." (1 Tim. 2:7).

*Prayer*: Dear Jesus, you said you are the way, the *truth*, and the light. Whenever you were asked questions by people who tried to mix you up (confuse you), you always confused them by telling the truth. Help us to be honest like you. Keep us from lying, even a tiny bit. Amen.

## Stubborn? Proud?

Sue Ellen had been very naughty. She had gone to a nearby park alone—a thing her mother had told her never to do. When Mother learned that she had disobeyed her, she sent Sue Ellen to her room.

"When you are ready to tell me you are sorry, you may come out and play," Mother said.

Sue Ellen stomped off to her room. She threw herself on her bed. Say she was sorry? She wouldn't! What she had done wasn't so bad. Other children went to the park alone.

Once Mother passed Sue Ellen's room. She stopped and waited in the doorway. But Sue Ellen pretended she didn't know she was there.

Time passed slowly. Sue Ellen read some of her picture books. She went to the window and watched the cars pass by on the street. But she would not tell her mother she was sorry for what she had done.

Sue Ellen heard her father come home from work. She heard him say, "Where's Sue Ellen?" Sue Ellen didn't hear her mother's answer, but she was sure she told her father what she had done.

Now Sue Ellen began to wish she had said she was sorry.

But as soon as the thought crossed her mind, she tightened her lips and shook her head. It would have been so much easier if she had said she was sorry right away. Now it would be much harder to do.

Soon Sue Ellen heard dinner noises. Still she stayed in her room. Then the sun set, and the room grew dark. Finally Sue Ellen slept—without telling her mother she was sorry.

*Something to Think About:* Why wouldn't Sue Ellen say she was sorry?

Could it be that she was a stubborn girl? Or was she proud? Pride can keep us from saying, "Please forgive me." It's very hard for some people to admit they have done wrong. When they fail to do this, they miss the good feeling that comes when things are made right again.

The next morning Sue Ellen crept out of her bed. She ran to her mother and threw her arms around her and kissed her. Mother believed this was her way to say she was sorry. But Sue Ellen never actually said those important words. It was then she set a pattern for her whole life. She grew up to be a woman who never liked to admit she was wrong. She always found it hard to say she was sorry for some wrong she had done.

*Bible Verse:* When the prodigal son, who had left home and fallen into sin, came back home he said, "Father, I have sinned against God and against you" (Luke 15:21).

In one of his psalms, David said, "I am sorry for my sins" (Ps. 38:18).

"If we confess our sins, he [God] is faithful and just to forgive us our sins and to cleanse us from all unrighteousness" (1 John 1:9).

"Let not the sun go down on your wrath [anger]" (Eph. 4:26).

*Prayer:* Dear Jesus, we know that when we ask you to forgive us, you always do. Help us always to admit our faults and our sins quickly. Don't let us go to bed angry. Help us make things right with the people we have wronged. Forgive us for the many times we have forgotten to say, "I'm sorry." In your blessed holy name, amen.

## Parrot Prayers

When Peter walked into the home of his Aunt Martha and his Uncle Charles, the first thing he heard was a shrill, squawking voice. "PollywantsacrackerHelloHelloPrettybird-Prettybird."

His aunt and uncle had a parrot! Green and yellow with a sharp, crossed beak and beady eyes!

"When did you get the parrot?" Peter asked.

"She really isn't ours," Aunt Martha answered. "We're taking care of her while our neighbors are on vacation."

"She talks funny."

"And fast," his aunt added.

Polly began to squawk again. "PrettybirdPrettybird-PollywantsacrackerNicegirlNicegirl."

Peter laughed and shook his finger at the parrot. "If you're talking to me, I want you to know I'm a boy, not a girl."

Polly didn't pay any attention. She squawked again, never stopping between words.

"That's parrot talk," Uncle Charles told Peter. "She has a good tongue but a poor brain."

At lunch Aunt Martha asked Peter to thank God for the food. He bowed his head, folded his hands and prayed, "AswebowingratitudeLordwethankyouforourfoodAmen."

When he looked up he saw that Aunt Martha and Uncle Charles were laughing at him.

"What's wrong?" he asked.

"You prayed a parrot prayer," Uncle Charles answered.

Peter understood. He hadn't realized before how fast he talked or that he really hadn't thought about the words he said. He was just like Polly.

"Better try again," Aunt Martha suggested.

Peter prayed again slowly, thinking about the meaning of every word.

*Something to Think About:* Do you ever pray as Peter did?

In church, do you ever find yourself singing a song without thinking about the meaning of the words?

Right now sing a song your family knows well. Talk about the meaning of the words of the song.

*Bible Verse:* "Whatever you do or say, let everything please the Lord" (Col. 3:17).

"I will pray with the spirit and will pray with understanding; I will sing with the spirit and I will sing with under-standing, too" (1 Cor. 14:15).

*Prayer:* Dear God in heaven, so often we pray without thinking about the meaning of the words. We just repeat words we have said before. Often we never think about meanings of words of songs we sing in church, either. Forgive us and help us to do and say everything so that we will please you. In Jesus' name, amen.

## When Everything Goes Wrong

Todd dragged his tired feet as he pushed his bicycle into the family garage. What a day! Everything had gone wrong. First he had overslept and been late for school. Besides, he forgot his arithmetic assignment at home.

At lunch he remembered he couldn't go home to eat. His father was taking his mother to their favorite restaurant to celebrate her birthday, and Todd hadn't taken any lunch money with him.

Then he had a flat tire. He'd have to fix it before dinner. *Before dinner?* Suddenly he remembered he had forgotten to pick up the birthday gift he had put on layaway for his mother. He had paid for it with his paper-route money. Now it was too late. The store was closed.

Todd let himself into the kitchen. There stood his mom and dad and Grandma Baines, laughing so hard tears spilled down their cheeks. Gift wrapping lay at his mother's feet. In her hand she held a cardboard poster.

"What's so funny?" he asked.

He must have sounded pretty sad because his father quit laughing long enough to say, "You certainly aren't. Had a bad day?"

"And how," Todd answered. Then he told his parents about his day.

Mother began laughing again. "Here." She gave the poster to Todd. "I think you need this gift more than I do. Dad bought it for me as a joke."

Todd looked at the poster. On it was a picture of a fat baby who had just dumped a bowl of spaghetti over his head. The bowl clung to his head like a cap. Spaghetti ran down his face and all over his clothes. Besides, he was crying as if his heart would break.

"Read the words at the bottom of the picture," Dad told Todd.

Todd read the words, printed in large letters: THIS IS THE DAY THE LORD HATH MADE . . . REJOICE AND BE GLAD IN IT (Ps. 118:24).

Todd looked at the picture again. The baby was a mess just as his day had been. . . .

"Rejoice! Be glad!" his mother said.

Again Todd looked at the picture. Then in spite of himself, he began to laugh. He laughed as hard as the rest of the family had.

*Something to Think About*: Some people think that when they become Christians they will never have any problems. Such thinking is wrong. We often cause our own problems. Would it be right for Todd to blame God for the things that had gone wrong in his day? Explain your answer.

We could say the baby on the poster had had a bad day. But what about the baby's mother? Hers must have been bad too.

Every day is a day given to us by God, whether it turns out to be good or bad. Either way we can be glad. We can thank and praise God because we know He will work out everything for good because we love Him.

*Bible Verse:* "This is the day the Lord has made, let us be glad and rejoice in it" (Ps. 118:24).

"In this world you will have trouble, but be of good cheer . . ." (John 16:33).

"He [God] will never fail you nor forsake you" (Josh. 1:5).

*Prayer:* Dear Lord Jesus, we can understand how Todd felt because we have had days just like his. Help us to remember that you give us each day and that we should be thankful even when things go wrong. We know we often cause our own problems. But we can always trust you to be with us. Help us to rejoice and be glad no matter what happens. Amen.

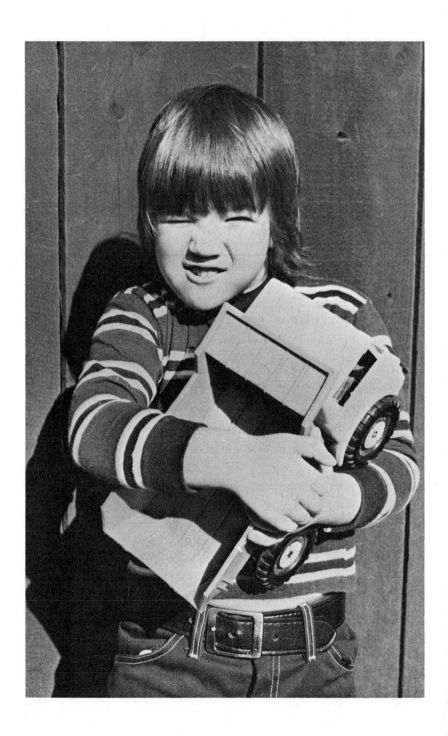

# Who Is Supposed to Share?

For his third birthday, Kent's parents bought him a shiny new dump truck.

As soon as he could, Kent hurried to tell his friends. They all thought the dump truck was one of the nicest presents a boy could get on his birthday. "We'll get our toys and come over and play in your sandbox," they told Kent.

As the boys played they hauled sand and built winding roads and tall buildings. Once during their play, Terry Palmer, who lived next door, turned to Kent. "Can I play with your dump truck for a little while?" he asked.

Kent grabbed his truck and wrapped his arms tightly around it. He shook his head.

"But we're supposed to share," Terry told him. But Kent wasn't in a sharing mood.

Some weeks later Terry had a birthday. His parents gave him a new tricycle. Terry rode his tryke back and forth on the sidewalk in front of Kent's home. Kent watched and wished he could ride it.

After lunch he decided to ask Terry if he could ride his tryke for a while. He hurried to the Palmer house and rang the doorbell. Mrs. Palmer answered the door.

"Can Terry come out and play with me?" he asked.

"I'm sorry. But Terry isn't home. He just went to the store with his father."

Kent wondered what he should do now. Then he had an idea.

"Then can Terry's new tryke come out and play with me?" he asked.

*Something to Think About:* What does the word *share* mean?

The dictionary has several meanings for the word. The ones that apply to this story say: *to enjoy with others; to use together.*

Did Kent have any right to expect Terry to let him ride his tryke?

Can you think of a Bible verse that Kent should remember?

*Bible Verse:* "Don't think only about yourself, but about others too" (Phil. 2:4).

"Whatever things you want others to do for you, you must also do for them" (Matt. 7:12).

*Prayer:* Dear Lord, we often forget what real sharing means. We expect others to share and then we don't share with them. Please forgive us. Thank you for sharing your Son, Jesus Christ, with us. We want to share our lives with Him. Help us not to think only of ourselves but of others too. Amen.

## Something to Grow Up To

For months Todd had looked forward to the day when he could start kindergarten. He talked about it all the time. He told everyone that soon he would be able to read and to write.

Finally the day came!

"Shall I go with you?" Mother asked.

Todd stood tall. "I can go by myself," he said.

Mother watched as he proudly marched off to school.

When he returned he didn't seem as excited as he had been before.

"Well, how did you like school?" Mother asked.

Todd wrinkled his nose, shrugged, and said, "Did you

172

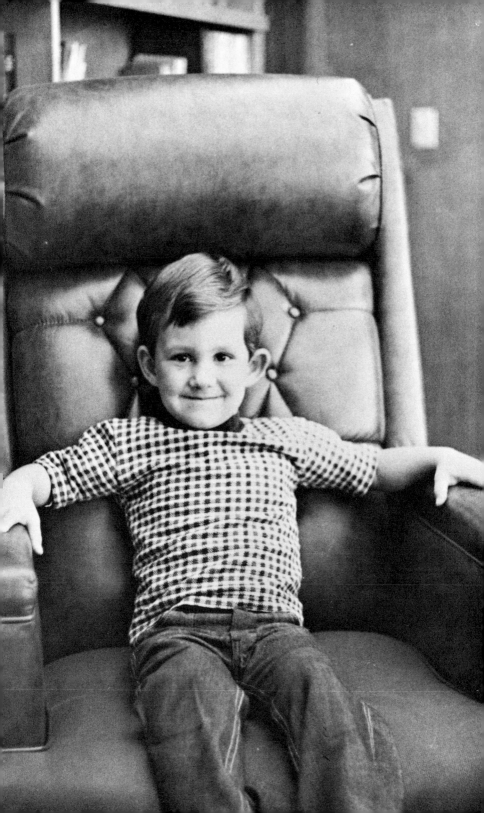

know they only have little chairs and tables my size?"

"Yes," Mother answered. "I knew that. Why do you ask?"

"Cause there's nothing to grow up to," Todd answered.

*Something to Think About:* We can be sure that the size of the chairs differed in each schoolroom, from kindergarten to first grade, second grade, and on up. The higher the grade, the bigger the chairs. But Todd didn't know this. Just the same, he said something that is important to remember. We all need something or someone to grow up to—something or someone we would like to be like.

What person would you like to grow up to be like? Why?

Who is your favorite Bible character? Whom do you respect and want to be like? Why?

What Bible verse helps you to be a better person?

*Bible Verse:* "Don't always be children . . . but speaking the truth in love, grow up to be like him [Jesus] in all things" (Eph. 4:15).

"He that walketh with wise men shall be wise" (Prov. 13:20).

*Prayer:* Dear Father in heaven, thank you for the Bible that tells us about people we can grow up to be like. Thank you for people today who are good examples to follow. Help us to choose the right people to grow up to. Help us to grow up to be like Jesus. Amen.

# Blabbermouth

Patty, who had been outside playing, came into the kitchen crying as if her heart would break. Mother turned away from the sink where she was washing dishes. She sat down and took her daughter into her lap. "Now, now," she said as she wiped the girl's tears. "What ever happened to you?"

"Donna called me 'Blabbermouth.'"

"Oh," Mother said. "I wonder why she did that? Do you know what a blabbermouth is?"

Patty swallowed hard. She nodded. "Someone who tells a secret."

"And did you tell a secret?"

Patty didn't answer for a long time. Then between sobs she said, "I told Judy that Donna stole one of Mr. McFarlan's apples."

"Did she?"

Again Patty nodded. "But her mother made her pay for it out of her allowance."

"Did she tell Mr. McFarlan she was sorry?"

"Her mother made her."

"I'm glad she did," Mother said. "But that doesn't change things for you, does it? Now what must you do?"

"Tell Donna I am sorry."

*Something to Think About:* Do you think Patty was a blabbermouth?

If Patty tells Donna she is sorry, will it make everything right?

Suppose Judy has already told another friend about the apple. This friend tells someone else. And that someone

175

else tells it to her friend. What happens then?

Trying to take back what we have said is like trying to pick up a bag full of feathers after the feathers have been scattered by the wind. It just can't be done.

So, what should we try always to do?

*Bible Verse:* "The tongue is a small thing but it can cause a lot of trouble. It's like a tiny spark that sets a whole forest of trees on fire" (James 3:5).

*Prayer:* Dear Jesus, you know how hard it is not to tell things we know. Please today help us to think before we speak. Don't let us be blabbermouths. Amen.

## And . . . Not Tell Daddy

One morning Mrs. Elvin gave her four-year-old daughter Carol a coin purse with a dollar bill in it. She asked her to go to the corner store and buy some raisins for a cake she was making.

Carol went to the store. When she came back, she handed Mother the raisins and the coin purse. The purse was empty. "Carol," she said, "wasn't there any change left over?"

Carol shook her head.

Mother lifted her daughter onto her lap. "Carol, you must tell me the truth. Where is the rest of the money?"

When Carol didn't answer, Mother said, "Open your hand, dear."

Slowly, ever so slowly, Carol opened her hand. There lay the money that was left after she had bought the raisins. "You didn't tell me the truth," Mother said. "You know that not telling the truth is wrong. But you can ask God to forgive you, and He will.

"And remember, dear, when God forgives a wrong, He forgets all about it."

Carol thought about what Mother had said. "Will you forget too?" she asked. "And . . . not tell Daddy?" she added quickly.

*Something to Think About:* If you had been Carol's mother, how would you have answered her?

Which is easier, to forgive or to forgive *and forget*?

*Bible Verse:* "If we confess [tell God] our sins, he is faithful and fair. He will forgive us . . . " (1 John 1:9).

"And their sins will I remember no more" (Heb. 8:12).

"I, even I [God], am he that blotteth out your sins . . . and will remember them no more" (Isa. 43:25).

*Prayer:* Dear God in heaven, thank you for forgiving us when we ask you to. And thank you, too, for forgetting things that we have done that were wrong. Help us to forget when someone asks us to forgive some wrong. Amen.

## Tumblina

Little Sue Paulson received a tumbling toy for Christmas. It looked like a ball, but it had a doll's head on top of it. No matter how much Sue pushed the doll around, it always came straight up again.

Mr. Paulson called the doll Tumblina. He said, "No matter how many times she tumbles over she comes up smiling."

*Something to Think About:* Tumblina has something to teach each one of us. No matter how many times mistakes, sickness, or trouble push us down, we, too, can come up smiling. A little chorus begins, "Rise and shine and give God the glory . . . ," which means get up, smile, and thank God for everything.

*Bible Verse:* "For we know that all things work together for good for those who love God" (Rom. 8:29).

*Prayer:* Dear Jesus, we know that we become better persons because life sometimes pushes us down. It is then we learn to trust you and to ask you to help us. When these things happen, help us to come up smiling. Amen.

## Be a Friend, Win a Friend

Stacy hated her new school. She wished she was back in Kelson where all her friends lived. "Why did Daddy have to get transferred anyway?" she muttered to herself.

She shuffled slowly along the sidewalk that led to the new school. She had been in the school for three days and no one had paid any attention to her. Oh, they stared at her when they first saw her, but then they'd look away and act as if she wasn't there.

At noon Stacy picked up her school lunch tray and began looking for a place to eat. She recognized three girls at a table where there was a vacant chair. They were in her history class. Stacy hesitated. *If only they would ask me to sit with them,* she thought. But they didn't.

Most of the tables were full. Finally Stacy found a table where a black girl sat all by herself. The girl looked up, smiled, then lowered her eyes quickly. *She looks lonesome,* Stacy thought.

"Hi," she said to the black girl. "I'm Stacy Martin. May I sit with you?"

"Oh, yes." The girl seemed pleased. "I was hoping you would."

Stacy set her tray down and pulled out a chair across the table from the girl.

"I'm Cornelia. I'm new here. I don't have any friends yet."

Stacy said, "I'm new too. I've been looking for a friend."

Cornelia laughed. "You've found one," she said.

*Something to Think About:* Have you ever been lonely?

Have you ever moved away from a city where you lived for a long time? How did you make new friends?

Why didn't the children in the new school speak to Stacy or the black girl and ask them to join them for lunch?

How do you treat newcomers in your school or in your church?

*Bible Verse:* "To have friends, a person must show that he is friendly" (Prov. 18:24).

*Prayer:* Dear Jesus, you are the best friend anyone can have. Thank you for being our friend. Help us always to be friendly to those who are lonely. Amen.

## Patty's Gold Star*

Patty came home from school carrying the paper on which she had drawn a picture of her hometown. Usually she would have clapped her hands when she smelled the cake Mother was baking. Today was different. She stomped through the kitchen and went directly to her room.

"Patty," Mother called. "Wait." But Patty didn't wait.

Mother hurried to her daughter's room. She found her sitting on her bed scowling at the paper she had brought home from school. "Whatever is the matter?" Mother asked.

---

* Adapted from a story written by the author for *My Sunday Reader.*

"I've decided I'm not going back to school. Not ever."

"And why not?"

Patty handed her mother the paper. Mother examined it carefully. "Looks pretty good to me," she said. "A little smudgy in the corner. But I like the airplanes flying like a flock of geese over the city. I like the post office and the grain elevators . . ."

"Teacher didn't like them."

"What makes you say that?"

"She didn't give me a gold star."

"So? She usually does . . ." She stopped and sniffed the air. "Oh, my!" she cried. "I forgot all about my cake. It must be burning."

Mother was right. The lovely cake was badly burned. "What a mess," she said. She looked at the cake sadly. "Well, if you aren't going to school anymore, you can be sure I'm never going to bake another cake."

Shocked, Patty cried, "Never bake another cake! But, Mother, you don't always burn cakes."

"That's right, and you don't always smudge your pictures."

Patty let the words sink into her mind. Slowly a smile spread across her face. Quietly she said, "I guess I'll go back to school tomorrow."

Mother nodded. "And I'll bake another cake. Right now. Want to help me?"

*Something to Think About*: What does this story teach you?

Someone has said, "If at first you don't succeed, try, try again." Why is this good advice?

None of us is perfect. Everyone makes mistakes. Because we do doesn't mean we should quit trying. Peter, one of Jesus' disciples, made a mistake when he denied that he knew Jesus. Sorry for his sin, he went on to prove that he did know and love Jesus.

*Bible Verse*: "I can do all things through Christ who gives me strength [help]" (Phil. 4:13).

*Prayer*: Dear Lord, we know we don't always act as we should. We make many mistakes. We are sorry. Please forgive us. Help us never to give up and quit trying to live as you want us to. Amen.

## Gram's Promise

When a favorite uncle died, Gary began to think about the meaning of death. It worried him a great deal even though he loved Jesus very much. He thought about his grandparents. They were much older than his uncle had been when he died. Gary didn't want Gram or Gramps to die, ever.

One day he told his grandmother how he felt. "Don't ever die, Gram, please, don't ever die."

Gram knelt beside him. She put her hands on his shoulders. "Gary," she said, "I promise. I'll never die."

Gary felt better for a time. Then he began to wonder if Gram would be able to keep her promise.

A year later, Gram did die. Gary couldn't understand it. She hadn't kept her promise.

A few days after the funeral, Gary made his way to the garden where his father was working. Quietly he stood and watched him for some time. He wondered if his dad felt as badly about Gram's death as he did.

"Dad, how come Gram died? She said she wouldn't ever die."

Father smiled. "She didn't."

"But she was buried . . ."

Father knelt and began digging in the dirt. "Come here, I want to show you something." He poked around in the ground until he found one of the seeds he had planted. "Look, Gary, I buried this seed in the ground. Do you know what had to happen to it before the new plant could begin to grow?"

Gary looked at the seed. The old covering had been pushed aside. A new plant had begun to grow.

"A seed has to die in order for it to have a new life," Father told him. "When we accept Christ as our Savior, our old sinful life has to die; then we are given a new life in Christ. Remember the verse, 'Old things have passed away, behold all things are made new'? This new life in us never dies.

"When Gram died her heart stopped beating, but her spirit left her body and went to be with God. Wherever Gram is she is still living."

"That's what she meant when she said she wouldn't die." Now Gary understood.

*Something to Think About:* What do you think? Do you think Gram really did keep her promise to Gary?

Why shouldn't we be afraid to die if we belong to Jesus?

*Bible Verse:* "Except a kernel of wheat falls into the ground and dies, it cannot have a new life. But if it dies, it grows and brings forth much fruit" (John 12:24).

"Blessed [happy] are the dead who died belonging to God" (Rev. 14:13).

"Even so, in Christ shall all be made alive" (1 Cor. 15:22).

"Whether we live or whether we die, we are with the Lord" (Rom. 4:8).

*Prayer:* Dear Jesus, we thank you for the new life you gave us when we turned our lives over to you. We know that because you rose from the dead, we will live again in heaven. Now we know we can say we will never die just as Gram did because our spirit, which belongs to you, never dies. Thank you, Lord, for your goodness and love that planned these things for us. Amen.

# Color Doesn't Count

When Scottie was a small boy, his minister father served an integrated (black and white) church in South Chicago. Since many of the white people had moved out of the area, most of the church members and Sunday school pupils were black. In fact, Scottie was the only white boy in his Sunday school class.

One day when Scottie's grandparents came to visit, Scottie showed them a picture of his Sunday school class.

"What a fine group of children," Grandma said.

"Can you find me?" Scottie asked excitedly. Then, not waiting for his grandparents to answer, he said, "There." He pointed to the place where he stood. "I'm the boy in the green shirt."

*Something to Think About:* Would Scottie have needed to tell his grandparents where he stood in the picture?

Did you notice he didn't say *I'm the white boy in the picture?* Why didn't he?

Could it be that thoughts about color never entered his mind? That he never thought of himself as being any different from his black friends?

In the Bible we have the words *whosoever, anyone, all, everyone,* which tell us God has no *favorite people* and that He loves everyone.

*Bible Verse:* "God is no respecter of persons [he has no favorites]" (Acts 10:34).

"Whosoever believes that Jesus is Christ is a child of God" (1 John 5:1).

*Prayer:* Dear Lord, thank you for the story about Scottie. If we had been in his place we might have said,

"I'm the white boy standing there." Help us not to think people of one color or race are better than another. Help us to love everyone as you do. Amen.

## Say "No!"

Charles and Wade were the best of friends. Both boys were Christians. Yet Charles seemed much more able to keep from being tempted than Wade.

Classmates hardly ever asked Charles to do things that he believed are wrong. But they pestered Wade all the time. "Come on, take a puff; it won't hurt you," they said when they tried to get him to smoke. Or, "What's the matter? Chicken?" Or, "Want to sneak into the movies with us tonight?"

Wade's problem was that he never really said *no*. He hesitated and then said, "Not this time." Or, "My folks would get mad." Or, "I don't think I should."

One day Charles scolded Wade for not standing up to the boys. "Tell them *no* once and for all. Say, 'Listen guys, I'm a Christian. Jesus lives in my life. Now stop bugging me. My answer is *no* and that's that!' That's what I did. And it works."

*Something to Think About:* Do your friends keep asking you to do things you know are wrong?

Try doing what Charles did. He's right. It does work.

Do this too. Decide right now what things you will say *no* to so you won't have to stop and think about them when temptation comes. Someone has said that many children and young people would never have taken drugs if they had decided beforehand to say "No!"

*Bible Verse:* "Don't swear by anything. But let your

*yes* be *yes* and your *no, no"* (James 5:12).

" . . . and be ready always to give an answer to every man who asks you why you believe as you do" (1 Pet. 3:15).

*Prayer:* Dear Lord, each of us is tempted in one way or another. We need your help in handling these temptations. Teach us what things we should decide right now to say *no* to. Help us to say *no* and mean it. Help us to live so that when people see how much we love you, they will stop trying to make us do wrong. Amen.

## Fifteen, Counting Jesus

Mary Jo's Sunday school class had a picnic. Three of the class mothers took the children and their teacher to the wild animal zoo for the day. What fun they had riding the train all over the place, watching lions, elephants, zebras, giraffes, monkeys, and birds of all kinds and colors.

Later they drove to a park to eat their picnic lunch.

When Mary Jo returned she told her mother all about the trip.

"How many were you altogether?" Mother asked.

"Sarah, Polly, Anne, George, Joe . . ." She began to name the children, the teachers, and the mothers, counting with her fingers. "Fourteen. No, fifteen, counting Jesus."

*Something to Think About:* You have learned that if we belong to Jesus, He is with us wherever we go—even on trips to wild animal zoos. He's with us when we are alone, at church, at school—everywhere. He goes with us because His Spirit lives in us.

*Bible Verse:* "Draw near to God and he will draw near to you" (James 4:8).

"And now, little children, abide [live with] him" (1 John 2:28).

"Lo, I am with you always, even to the end of the world" (Matt. 28:20).

"Where two or three are gathered together in my name, there am I in the midst of them" (Matt. 18:20).

*Prayer*: Dear Jesus, it's good to know that you are with us wherever we go. We need your Holy Spirit to help us act as we should in school, at home, in church, and on picnics and trips. Help us to stay near to you so that you can stay near to us. Amen.

## Who Do Men Say That You Are?

Very early one morning, Lowell knocked on his parents' bedroom door. "Who is it?" Father asked.

"It's me, Lowell," Lowell answered. "It's raining awfully hard. Will you or Mom take the car and come with me on my paper route?"

"I will," Mother answered. "You father needs his sleep. He has a hard day ahead of him. I'll be with you in a minute."

Mother dressed quickly. When she stepped into the hall, she found her two younger children, Trevor and Cindy, dressed in their raincoats, waiting for her.

"Can we go too?" Trevor asked.

"Such children!" Mother said. "Oh, I suppose you can. But you have to promise to be quiet and to sit still in the car."

Mother drove the car slowly and carefully through the pouring rain to the place where Lowell picked up his papers, folded them, and put them in long wax bags so they wouldn't get wet. Then Mother drove to the section of the city where Lowell's route was located.

Trevor and Cindy sat very still. They didn't talk much either. Lowell didn't give them a chance! Whenever he delivered a paper to a house, he told his mother, Trevor, and Cindy about the people who lived there.

"They've got a mean teenager there," Lowell said, pointing to the home where he had just delivered a paper. "Once I heard him grumble and sass his mother when she asked him to mow the lawn."

"I like the man who lives in that second-floor apartment. Once I threw a paper too hard. It hit the deck lamp and broke it. When I went up to tell the man I'd pay for it, he wouldn't let me. He seemed surprised that I had told him I broke the lamp. He said, 'I like an honest kid.' "

"She's stingy. She never has money ready when I come to collect. Sometimes I have to go back three or four times before she pays me."

"And those people. They're Christians, I'm sure. They have a picture of Jesus hanging above their fireplace."

On the way home, Cindy asked, "How come you know so much about these people?"

Lowell shrugged his shoulders. "I guess I just can't help but know a lot about them because I see them so often. I know what they say and how they act."

"Humm," Mother said thoughtfully. "That makes me wonder."

"About what?" Trevor asked.

"About our paper boy. I wonder what he thinks about us?"

*Something to Think About:* Mother knew that we don't live only to please ourselves. People all around watch what we do.

**What do you suppose your paper boy thinks about you? Or your mailman? Or your garbage collector? Does it matter?**

*Bible Verse:* "Don't let any man think little of you because you are young: but be an example to others by the way you talk and act. Let them see by your faith, your love, and your clean life that you love Jesus" (1 Tim. 4:12).

"By this shall all men know that you are my disciples, if you love one another" (John 13:35).

*Prayer:* Dear Jesus, we know that none of us can hide what we do. People who meet us know what we are like by how we act and talk. Help us to be careful how we speak. Help us to show by our clean lives that we love and believe in you. Amen.